The Right Balance
Provision for Slow Learners
in Secondary Schools

Louise Clunies-Ross and
Shirley Wimhurst

NFER-NELSON

Published by The NFER-NELSON Publishing Company Ltd.,
Darville House, 2 Oxford Road East,
Windsor, Berks, SL4 1DF

First published 1983
© NFER
ISBN 0-7005-0555-5
Code 8092 02 1

All rights reserved. No part of this publication may be
reproduced or transmitted, in any form or by any means,
without permission.

Filmset in Plantin by Cambrian Typesetters,
Aldershot, Hampshire.
Printed in Great Britain

Distributed in the USA by Humanities Press Inc.,
Atlantic Highlands, New Jersey 07716 USA.

Contents

List of Tables

List of Appendices

Acknowledgements

This NFER-sponsored research was supervised throughout by Miss Margaret Reid to whom we are grateful for advice and guidance, in particular for her assistance with questionnaire design and for her valuable criticism of the text in preparation.

It is with regret that we cannot name those in the schools who made this research possible, but we extend grateful thanks to all the heads and teachers who participated in the project by writing to us, by completing questionnaires or by welcoming us into their schools. In this regard we are especially indebted to the head teachers and staff of the seventeen schools in which we carried out case studies; their willing help and support was much appreciated.

We thank Miss Gillian Perry for her research contribution during the first 12 months of the project and in particular for her investigation into teacher training courses. Our thanks go to Miss Janet May and the NFER library staff for their support and especially to Mrs Susan Hancock who assisted us so well in the compilation of a test bibliography. We are grateful to NFER Statistical Services and Mr Peter Smedley for processing the computerized questionnaire data and to Mrs June Richardson for her careful help in coding and preparing the data. Our thanks to Mrs Linda Mount and Mrs Ann Symmonds who ably provided the project's secretarial support and to Mrs Anne Watson and Mrs Sheena McDermott who gave additional assistance in the typing of the final draft of this report.

I would also like to thank Mrs Shirley Wimhurst, who joined the project as assistant research officer for the final 15 months, for her enthusiasm and hard work during this time, which made it possible to undertake a concentrated programme of fieldwork. Shirley compiled Chapters three, six and seven of this report while the remaining chapters were the work of the principal author, who also edited the final draft.

Louise R. Clunies-Ross
August 1982
NFER, Slough

Chapter one

Introduction

1.1 Who are the Slow Learners?

This report is the outcome of a survey conducted during the autumn
of 1979, which was followed by a series of visits to secondary schools
in 15 local education authority areas throughout England and Wales
during 1980 and 1981. Information was gathered from a sample of
791 non-selective secondary schools drawn from within every LEA
and located in urban, inner city, suburban and rural areas. The
marked differences in the nature of the school populations thus
identified posed a research problem which was summarized as
follows by a participating head teacher:

> As always there are difficulties in classifying 'slow learners'.
> Where the quality of intakes varies widely between schools it
> becomes difficult to determine the cut-off level below which
> pupils receive special provision and hence the subsequent
> decision as to how much of the school's resources ought to be
> directed toward this area.

Other aspects of this problem were apparent. The head of one
school wrote:

> Who are the slow learners? I have drawn a deliberate distinction
> between 'slow learners' and 'remedials' on the basis that all
> remedials are slow learners but that the reverse does not apply.

while the head teacher of another school explained:

> The distinction between 'slow learner' and a learner in need of
> remedial attention on a specific aspect of learning is a problem

which besets the specialist teacher of slow learners and has implications for pupil grouping and deployment of staff resources.

The problem was further complicated by local conditions, such as those experienced by the head from north Wales who commented that 'an important factor affecting the teaching of slow learners in this school is the English/Welsh linguistic divide'. In a northern city, one head teacher wrote of 'the problem of immigrant children who are not dull but who need specialist help with language'; in his school one pupil in seven required such assistance.

Since head teachers and their staff were those best placed to assess the learning needs of pupils in the schools, it was resolved to call upon their expertise in identifying slow learning pupils, i.e. responses were to be invited which would reflect the situation in one school with a particular intake and a specific set of resources at a given point in time. Thus, the school's definition of what was perceived to be a slow learning pupil constituted an essential and integral part of the research design.

The problem of definition is not new. Gulliford (1969) suggests that the slow learner is a pupil in an ordinary school rather than in a special school, making the distinction between slow learners and educationally subnormal pupils. Williams (1970) uses the term for 'those children who are of limited intelligence', excluding the underachieving more able pupil. Both of these descriptions refer to the population on which our inquiry focused; a group of pupils whom Brennan (1974) describes as 'those pupils who are unable to cope with the school-work normal for their age group but whose failure to do so cannot be explained by the presence of any handicapping condition'. He continues with the words that 'should any such condition be present in a pupil who is to be regarded as a slow learner, then it will be in marginal form only and clearly secondary to the learning difficulty which is the primary cause of school failure'. While this remains a somewhat general definition, it is evident that within its compass are found slow learning pupils who exhibit a wide range of differing educational needs.

1.2 Background to the Research

The research took place twelve years after HM Inspectorate investigated the arrangements made for slow learning pupils in 158 secondary schools in England; their findings, published in 1971 as Education Survey 15, identified 'a widespread uncertainty of aims, objectives and methods for slow learners in many − indeed the majority − of the schools visited' (DES, 1971). Moreover, in a period of rapid educational change, it was reported that 'the needs of the slowest pupils seem to have received less than their fair share of consideration' and that there was 'uncertainty about the nature of their potential, the nature and extent of their disabilities, the most appropriate organization, suitable educational methods and techniques and about the nature of a suitable curriculum'. The Inspectors concluded that there was much to be done 'before the needs of the slow learners in secondary schools can be said to be satisfactorily met' (op. cit.).

Since the publication of Education Survey 15 there have been far-reaching changes in secondary education, some of which have brought issues concerned with the education of the less academically gifted into sharper focus.

With the spread of reorganization and the establishment of comprehensive schools many more head teachers are faced with decisions as to how best to provide for the less able pupils in the new intake. On what criteria should pupils be selected to receive special or supplementary teaching? How should provision for such pupils be organized? What form should the curriculum take? For how many years should special provision be made available?

The introduction of mixed ability groups during the 1970s presented further problems. In 1976 the NFER team investigating mixed ability teaching in secondary schools found that problems associated with the education of slow learning pupils were among those most commonly raised by the 500 heads and assistant teachers interviewed. How could class teachers, without extra assistance, best provide for the needs of slow learners in the group? In what ways could special help be made available to slow learners in a mixed ability class? What resource materials and teaching techniques were most appropriate for less able pupils? (Reid *et al.*, 1981)

Confronting both heads and teachers were issues of school organization. Should slow learning pupils be the responsibility of one special department or should the responsibility be shared among several or all departments? Should slow learners be taught in a 'remedial' department or should they be integrated with the mainstream? How best could advice and guidance about pupils' specific learning difficulties be presented to teachers? To what extent should the role of remedial staff be an advisory one? What lines of communication could be set up to strengthen links not only between staff but with service agencies beyond school?

The aim of the NFER-sponsored research was to address the questions posed above and to explore the issues in detail, providing within the report an information source on which staff seeking to establish or to review provision for slow learning pupils might draw to aid their decision making.

By 1980 a further change was affecting schools in the secondary sector. Falling pupil rolls and consequent reductions in the staffing establishment had resulted in a number of school mergers and closures. These combined with financial cutbacks were beginning to have an effect on some schools in the sample. The two years between the autumns of 1979 and 1981 had seen changes in staffing and in school organization which had resulted in the support available to slow learners being reduced in several schools. The project team was aware that the situation being monitored was in a state of change throughout the three academic years involved; not only were heads and their staffs constantly reviewing, evaluating and adapting the provision made in an effort to provide the best possible support for slow learning pupils, but in a period of financial restraint it was more than usually apparent that such review was taking place at a time of contraction rather than expansion in education. The most economical ways of maintaining adequate provision for slow learners were being sought in terms of staff deployment, resource production and the allocation of teaching spaces and equipment.

1.3 Outline of Previous Research

There had been four previous surveys of slow learner provision at the time the project began in 1979 and the National Association for Remedial Education (NARE) subsequently carried out a survey of remedial teachers in 1980. All of these surveys were much smaller in scale than the NFER research.

The DES survey of 158 comprehensive and secondary modern schools, undertaken in the late 1960s, identified a diversity of practice in the organization of provision for slow learners. Head teachers estimated that between 7 and 16 per cent of their pupils on the school roll needed some measure of specialized help, and that just over half of these were currently being catered for. It was agreed that the term 'slow learner' lacked definition and that careful diagnosis and assessment of the nature of the difficulties experienced by slow learners was required, if schools were to make suitable provision. HMI drew attention to the fact that many pupils with limited intellectual attainments also had other problems, of which physical or sensory handicaps, maladjustment and social deprivation were the most common. Education Survey 15 recommended that systematic arrangements be made at transition to ensure that pupils with special needs did not suffer when transferring from junior to secondary school.

At the time of the survey in the late 1960s, most schools grouped all pupils into streams or bands according to ability. One-third of the schools had a special department for slow learning pupils and most of these had a head of department, but heads reported difficulties in recruiting suitable qualified and experienced teachers for these posts. It was felt that limited opportunities for specialist training and poor teaching facilities deterred staff from taking up remedial work. Few of the teachers surveyed had specific training for work with slow learners. In the remaining two-thirds of the schools surveyed, the slowest pupils were taught in special classes or groups, or offered 'remedial sessions' within the school or at outside centres; half of these schools had a graded post available for the teacher with special responsibility for slow learners.

Eighty-nine per cent of the schools surveyed by the Inspectorate had received some help from the support services in dealing with the learning and other difficulties of their pupils. The schools' psychological service, educational welfare officers and school medical officers were the services most frequently mentioned, but staff felt that the general shortage of specialist advice gave cause for anxiety.

HMI reported that there was an urgent need to make a critical examination of the curriculum offered to slow learners and stressed that the needs of the majority were not necessarily fulfilled by specialized help in reading, writing and arithmetic, nor were they met by exposing slow learners to a full programme of specialist subject teaching. HMI recommended the implementation of a specially designed, integrated curriculum which took account of pupils' individual differences, to be taught by resourceful and imaginative staff.

In 1970, Sampson and Pumfrey undertook a questionnaire survey of 270 comprehensive and secondary modern schools, exploring the organization of remedial education and the deployment, status and characteristics of those staff who taught slow learners. The results closely reflected those reported by HMI in every aspect except organization. In contrast to the 33 per cent identified by HMI, Sampson and Pumfrey found that in 90 per cent of schools remedial education was the responsibility of a special department staffed mainly by full-time teachers who concentrated on teaching reading, English and maths to classes, groups or individual pupils, using a variety of teaching approaches. However, as previously noted, specialized accommodation for slow learners was rare and only 25 per cent of remedial staff were trained to teach slow learners. The number of pupils with learning difficulties catered for within the schools ranged from four per cent to 27 per cent of the school roll, and little distinction was made between 'slow learners', 'backward' and 'remedial' pupils. The researchers recommended that research into remedial arrangements should take place, since 'currently, opinion and convenience rather than researched fact appear to exert undue influence' (Sampson and Pumfrey, 1970).

The Welsh Secondary Schools Association's enquiry into remedial education, carried out during the spring of 1977, reported extremely varied provision for slow learners. The survey found that slow learning children were usually taught in remedial classes or extracted groups and that a large number of the 275 comprehensive and secondary modern schools in the enquiry used both methods (Athey, 1978). Information was gathered on the organization, staffing, testing and resourcing of provision for slow learners.

Approximately 90 per cent of schools had a slow learner department, of which over half had a head of department appointed on scale 3 or above. While special classes and extraction played a major part in the organization of remedial education, extraction was favoured by smaller schools and remedial classes by larger schools with more than 900 pupils on roll. The survey reported an increased number of remedial teachers relative to the slow learner population as compared with data in previous surveys. One-third of remedial staff had received special training, and 64 per cent of heads of department had an advanced qualification in remedial or special education.

Research by the Schools Council 'Curricular Needs of Slow

Learners' project again identified 'the separate special class' and 'withdrawal from ordinary class for special teaching' among the 183 participating secondary schools (Brennan, 1979). Brennan recorded widespread concern for the welfare of slow learners but warned that this was in danger of ousting educational objectives involving knowledge, skills and cognitive processes. He urged teachers to accept the involvement of parents and the community in the development and implementation of an appropriate curriculum for slow learners.

The most recent survey was carried out by NARE during 1980 and some preliminary results became available in 1981. Remedial teachers indicated that a wider interpretation of their role might be emerging as very few were concerned solely with teaching literacy to slow learners; almost half were involved in teaching social and life skills, and a number were expected to advise other staff on various educational issues including slow learners and 'the bright under-achiever'. Major research was now needed, reported Gains and McNicholas, to validate these emerging trends (TES, 11 September, 1981).

1.4 The NFER Provision for Slow Learners Project

The research was planned in two main phases. The first, from January 1979 to September 1980 comprised the design, administration and analysis of a postal questionnaire which was sent to the heads of a 20 per cent sample of maintained secondary schools in England and Wales. A follow-up questionnaire was subsequently sent to teachers of slow learners in these schools. The schools were selected by computer to provide a random sample which was representative in terms of size and location, of all maintained comprehensive, modern, bilateral, technical and middle deemed secondary schools in England and Wales. The sample included both junior and senior high schools but excluded 6th form colleges, since the research was focusing on the years of compulsory education. The second major phase of the research took the form of a series of intensive case studies in secondary schools which were chosen to exemplify the different ways in which slow learner provision might be organized. Case studies were carried out between October 1980 and May 1981, leaving the remaining months of 1981 for the preparation of the research report.

Questionnaire Survey

A substantial two-part questionnaire was sent to the head teachers of 931 secondary schools in September 1979. The first section, focusing on school policy and organization, was designed for completion by the head teacher while the second, which requested details of school type, size, staffing, pupil grouping and the organizational structure of slow learner provision, could readily be delegated to a senior staff member for completion.

The response rate of 85 per cent (791 replies) was most encouraging. Data were received from 93 middle and 698 other secondary schools. Many heads enclosed school handbooks, prospectuses and documents concerned with slow learner provision to support the questionnaire information and five out of six expressed a wish to participate in the next stage of the research. Comments on teacher training and recruitment made it clear that these were areas of particular concern to head teachers and it was therefore decided to incorporate in the project a brief survey of initial and in-service training courses currently available for those who wished to teach slow learners in secondary schools.

The follow-up questionnaire, designed for those schools where heads had indicated a wish for further involvement, was sent to 661 schools in the summer term of 1980. The head of department or teacher in charge of slow learner provision was asked to provide details of group sizes and accommodation, and to give information on tests and teaching materials used. Short questionnaires were included, for completion by each member of staff who was known to spend a substantial part of the week teaching slow learning pupils. Responses were received from 68 per cent of teachers in charge of slow learner provision (447 schools) and individual staff returned teacher questionnaires from a further 18 schools. In total, 1467 teacher questionnaires were analysed, providing details of teacher training, subject background, teaching experience and participation in in-service courses in addition to information about length of service and the nature and status of a teacher's present appointment.

School Case Studies

Visits were made to a number of schools in order to verify

questionnaire data and to establish initial guidelines on case study structure before the main programme began in the autumn of 1980. The seventeen schools which were selected for intensive study exemplified the different forms of slow learner provision identified from questionnaire data. The classes, sets and withdrawal groups in which special provision was made for slow learners are described in detail in Chapter two. Other kinds of provision available in many of these schools, but which were not used as major variables, included special slow learner options and the use of peripatetic remedial staff, support teachers, volunteer parents and 6th form students.

Visits to schools were usually made for a period of four working days, in which discussion, interviews and periods of classroom observation took place. The intake year group was selected for intensive study, since this consisted of pupils for whom the staff had to make decisions about placement and about special provision where this was deemed necessary. Prior to each visit, the teacher in charge of slow learner provision was asked to select a 'typical slow learner' in the intake year who was to be the subject of the classroom observation studies. It was requested that the selected pupil, boy or girl, did not have additional problems such as maladjustment; after several visits a further proviso was added to the effect that the pupil's first language should be English, since it was observed that the problems of some slow learners were exacerbated by the fact that English was not their mother tongue.

The pupil, who was not told that he or she was being observed, was watched in every lesson throughout one day. Records were made of the kinds of tasks set by teachers and of the nature of the responses made by the pupil. Particular note was kept of how long a slow learner spent on a given task, what resource materials were associated with different kinds of tasks and what appeared to cause the pupil to stop work or become diverted from it before the set task was completed. A note was made of the pupil's interaction with peers and with the teacher – the frequency and the nature of such interactions were recorded together with details of the teaching strategies employed at the time – and the nature and availability of resource materials. At the team's request the observation day included lessons in English, maths and, in many cases, a science and a practical subject such as art, metalwork or music. The slow learner was observed in both special and mainstream groups and all staff who taught the pupil during the day provided contextual and background information about the observed lessons and commented on any features which were new or unusual as far as the observed pupil was concerned. The presence of the non-participant observers was considered to have a negligible effect on the pupils' behaviour, although a few teachers reported that children were a little more subdued than usual. Where 'reading mums', 6th form helpers or support teachers were normally present in the classroom, no change was made in arrangements and their role was noted, with special reference to any help given to the observed pupil. Throughout all observations it was stressed that the normal routine should continue and teachers should not alter their planned programme in any way.

Timetables were obtained from each observed pupil, together with timetables from others in the same year group who did not receive remedial help, so that an analysis of the curricular content offered to the two groups could be made. Background information on each observed pupil was gathered from school records so that the team had basic reference data on age, previous academic progress and any special problems which the pupil had experienced prior to entry. In schools where special courses were available for 4th and 5th year pupils, observers sat in on some of the lessons and subsequently discussed the aims and content of the course with the staff concerned, noting how far teachers felt they were succeeding in achieving their aims by this method of special provision for older pupils.

Each case study included a discussion with the head in which matters of school policy and staffing were explored, together with other specific issues raised by the original questionnaire. Any changes which had taken place since the initial contact was made were monitored and future plans for the development of slow learner provision discussed. The teacher in charge of slow learning pupils was interviewed concerning the the aims and objectives of the school's system of special educational provision. The ways in which pupils' needs were diagnosed and the curriculum and teaching methods employed to meet them were investigated and the nature of the role of the teacher in charge of slow learner provision was explored in depth.

During the spring term, staff in case study schools were asked to administer a reading test to the whole of the intake year, i.e. the year group which was monitored by the team. This was necessary in order to establish a common base line with regard to those pupils identified as 'slow learners' in the wide range of catchment areas represented by participating schools. Sixteen of the seventeen case study schools took part and provided the project with scores derived from the *Spar Reading Test*.

1.5 The Structure of the Report

The research project therefore gathered two quite different kinds of data. The first, derived from the wide sample of schools, provided an indication of the policies and organizational strategies adopted country-wide, and the second, resulting from detailed case studies, explored the implications of particular strategies for both teacher and pupil. The chapters which follow draw on both sources of information. Chapter two focuses on the ways in which schools organize provision for slow learning pupils, exploring the different kinds of pupil groupings employed and their associated benefits and disadvantages as perceived by heads and teachers. The practices of all 791 schools are included in this survey, from which a few of the more widely used systems are selected as examples.

Chapter three investigates how teachers in case study schools identified slow learning pupils in each new intake and explores the part played by the head of the remedial department or the teacher in charge of slow learners in the placement of such pupils into teaching, withdrawal and registration groups. Test results are used to illustrate the differing percentages of pupils aged 11+ with low reading ages who were present in the schools visited and examples are used to show how many of these pupils were given remedial help by means of different systems of provision.

In Chapter four an account is given of those staff who spent a major part of their week teaching slow learners in survey schools throughout the country. Information gained from questionnaires is used to provide details of their subject background, initial training and teaching experience. The chapter also includes details of staff appointments and timetables, comments on in-service education courses which focused on slow learners and information on staff membership of professional associations concerned with the education of slow learners. Following on from this section, Chapter five explores in some detail the role of the head of department or teacher in charge of slow learning pupils in the case study schools visited.

Involvement in assessment, diagnosis, prescription, teaching, staff support and liaison are discussed together with participation in policy formulation at management level and advisory work with mainstream subject teachers.

Chapter six explores the nature of the curriculum offered to slow learners in case study schools, focusing on the 11+ to 13+ age group. With the aid of specific examples the implications of particular school policies for both teacher and slow learning pupil are investigated with particular reference to the curriculum, resources, pupil grouping and teaching strategies adopted. Chapter seven contains details of the curriculum and special courses offered to slow learners in the 4th and 5th years and also describes other opportunities made available to this age group using outside resources. Again, examples are used to illustrate the major points raised. The final chapter draws together the main findings from this research, identifying major trends and suggesting ways in which schools might best deploy both staff and resources in order to make provision for the needs of slow learning pupils.

Chapter two

The Organization of Provision for Slow Learners

The main question is whether we ought to segregate slow learners from their social peers and thus emphasize their situation. This must be balanced against their educational need. (Head of a middle school)

The dilemma of whether to withdraw from groups in the mainstream or to separate off slow learners into their own group remains. Can research provide any guidelines? (Secondary school head)

2.1 Introduction

These questions highlight the dilemma facing head teachers who are responsible for both formulating and implementing school policy concerning the education of slow learning pupils and for organizing provision so that the best possible match between perceived needs and available resources is achieved. However provision for slow learners might be organized, there are obvious implications for staffing, resource materials and the allocation of curricular time; decisions must also be made regarding the size of teaching groups, for example, the nature of the syllabus, and perhaps the place of team teaching and mechanisms for in-class support. This is a difficult task and this chapter sets out to detail some of the ways in which special provision for slow learners has been organized, to explore some of the reasons why heads adopted these methods and to examine, through the eyes of the practitioners the perceived strengths – and weaknesses – of specific systems. Our research indicated that these systems were constantly under surveillance and that the provision made for slow learners was likely to change from one academic year to the next. This was in part a response to the changing needs of slow learning pupils and in part the result of an ongoing evaluation process.

Deliberately, the team did not set out to 'define' a slow learning pupil; first, because this would have involved extensive, time-consuming testing programmes in all 791 schools, and second, because the research ought to establish how school staff identified slow learners and how such pupils were subsequently catered for. The many different ways in which slow learning pupils were identified are discussed fully in Chapter three; in this chapter we explore the organizational structure within which teachers worked to try to meet pupils' educational needs.

Information was elicited from a section of the questionnaire which focused on the organization of provision for slow learners. First, descriptions were given of four commonly adopted forms of pupil grouping and heads were asked to indicate which, if any, were used in their schools in order to make educational provision for slow learners.

A special slow learner class was defined as 'a group of pupils identified by the school as slow learners and taught together for more than one subject'. Such a class might be taught by either remedial or subject specialists.

A slow learner set was distinguished from a class as 'a group of pupils identified on subject-specific criteria as slow learners, taught together for a particular subject'. An explanatory note stated that while a school might offer a number of subject-specific sets, a positive response to this question indicated the presence of at least one.

The term 'slow learner option' was used to describe a group of pupils identified by the school as slow learners who were taught together for a specially designed subject option, and a positive response indicated the availability of at least one special option for slow learners.

A withdrawal system referred to a situation in which pupils identified as requiring support in basic skills or in specific subjects were withdrawn from the mainstream for periods of individual or small group teaching.

In addition, heads were invited to outline alternative or additional systems employed within the school to cater for the needs of slow learning pupils and to describe any special arrangements made for 6th form pupils with learning difficulties. In every case, details of the year groups involved were requested so that slow learner provision could be seen against the background of the organization of the whole school. Questionnaire data were supplemented in many cases by school handbooks and by some documentation specific to slow learner provision, while the case studies enabled a closer examination to be made of the implications of particular systems for both pupil and teacher.

2.2 Main Forms of Organization

Six out of every seven head teachers combined the forms of grouping outlined above to create a variety of different systems of slow learner provision within their schools. The most widely used method of providing extra or alternative tuition for slow learners was by withdrawal from the mainstream for individual or small group teaching. Pupils identified as requiring support in basic skills or in specific subjects were withdrawn for this purpose in 85 per cent of secondary schools. Withdrawal took place in all year groups and from all kinds of classes. This, of course, has widespread implications for curriculum, teaching methods and teacher liaison as well as for the pupil, who might be rejoining a special slow learner class, a mixed ability group, a subject set or a streamed teaching unit. Pupils were withdrawn for remedial tuition slightly more often in the lower school than in the 4th and 5th years. Subject specific sets for slow learning pupils were present in 73 per cent of schools, constituting the second most widely adopted form of organization. More schools provided slow learner sets in the upper school as part of the whole school's setting and option system than in the lower school, where slow learner sets were often only organized for literacy and/or numeracy skills. Slow learner classes — the third most widely pracised form of slow learner provision — were adopted by 55 per cent of schools and were twice as commonly organized in the lower school (11+ to 13+) as in the upper (14+ and 15+). Fifty-two per cent of schools provided options designed specifically for slow learners and as expected these were most usually available in the 4th and 5th years. However, it was found that one in seven of these schools offered a special slow learner option to younger pupils.

Thirteen per cent of schools employed other means of providing for slow learners in addition to those already described above: for example, arranging for volunteer parents or 6th formers to hear pupils read on a one-to-one basis, timetabling 'floating' teachers to work in mainstream lessons, setting up reading, spelling and handwriting groups, arranging counselling facilities, and using the local Reading Centre. All of these systems and more were used to supplement other forms of slow learner provision in ten per cent of secondary and 30 per cent of middle schools deemed secondary.

Extra help for 6th year pupils was available in 26 per cent of the schools with 6th form students, and usually took the form of individual coaching for those with spelling, handwriting and language problems. Several heads reported that this had proved particularly helpful for pupils whose second language was English. In some schools a special 6th form group had been set up for pupils who wished to re-sit CSE examinations.

The way in which each of these organizational strategies is used, either uniquely or in combination with one or more of the other forms of provision, can be seen in Table 2.1 which shows the 14 different types of slow learner provision made in the secondary schools surveyed and the ten systems adopted within middle schools deemed secondary. (The latter, for simplicity, are henceforth referred to as 'middle schools'.)

There were only three secondary schools in which no special provision for slow learners was made; two heads stated that they had no slow learners on roll and the third organized sets for all pupils and hence made no additional provision for slow learners. All of the middle schools made some provision for slow learning pupils.

Finding ways of making special help available to slow learners was of obvious concern to head teacers and their staff and Table 2.1 illustrates the many different ways in which resolution of this problem was attempted. The dilemma facing schools is well reflected in the following quotations:

HMI report that remedial classes remove the less able from the company of their contemporaries for too much of the week, even though the work of the remedial class can be more easily integrated and designed to meet their needs exclusively. (*Ten Good Schools*, 1977)

Table 2.1: *Organization of provision for slow learners*

Type of Provision	Secondary	Schools Middle Deemed Secondary	Total	%
	N	N		
Class only	16	4	20	(3)
Set only	15	3	18	(2)
Withdrawal only	56	11	67	(8)
Class + Set	18	2	20	(3)
Class + Option	9	–	9	(1)
Class + Withdrawal	43	3	46	(6)
Set + Option	8	–	8	(1)
Set + Withdrawal	79	43	122	(16)
Option + Withdrawal	33	1	34	(4)
Class + Set + Option	41	–	41	(5)
Class + Set + Withdrawal	71	16	87	(11)
Class + Option + Withdrawal	37	–	37	(5)
Set + Option + Withdrawal	100	3	103	(13)
Class + Set + Option + Withdrawal	169	7	176	(22)
No provision for slow learners	3	–	3	(neg.)
	698	93	791	(100)

A withdrawal system, on the other hand,

> while it can help to remedy specific weaknesses of backward children, can provide too little support for the dull or severely retarded who on return to their normal class tend to flounder. (*Statistics of Education*, 1977a)

Both organizational methods are open to criticism and clearly there are advantages and disadvantages in both systems. The variety of ways in which schools made provision for slow learners by combining two or more different kinds of organization demonstrates teachers' awareness of the implications of each of the systems for pupils at different stages in their development and highlights the efforts made to cater for pupils with a range of learning difficulties.

In some secondary schools, for example, special classes were provided from entry up to and including the 5th year; in others, classes were available for the first three years after which slow learners were catered for by a withdrawal system, special options or sets. Other systems displayed quite different patterns, with slow learners withdrawn in the lower school (years 1 to 3 only), and joining special sets or options in the 4th and 5th years. Many schools made more than one type of special help available to slow learning pupils in each year group; special classes existed alongside a withdrawal system in many schools and special options as well as sets were frequently offered to slow learners in the 4th and 5th years, sometimes in addition to withdrawal.

In middle schools — the majority of which catered for pupils aged between nine and 13 — it was found that half provided sets plus a withdrawal system for slow learners and a further one in every five organized a special class as well. It was not usual to find more than two forms of special provision available in any year group. Under the age of 11, more pupils were given help by means of withdrawal procedures than by any other method, while the majority of slow learners in the 11+ age group were provided with both sets and a withdrawal facility. A minority were taught in special slow learner classes and very few were offered specially designed options. Where options existed, most were modern language alternatives.

In the sections which follow, an evaluation of each method of catering for the needs of slow learning pupils is made by its practitioners, and the ways in which different kinds of provision can interlock to provide a specific programme for slow learners are explored.

2.3 Head Teachers' Views on the Major Forms of Pupil Grouping for Slow Learner Provision

Separate classes for slow learners, which were organized in 436 schools, were present in almost two-thirds of secondary and in one-third of middle schools. In only 20 schools, however, did these constitute the sole form of special provision available.

The most frequently cited reason for organizing separate classes was to provide the opportunity for slow learning pupils to be taught in small groups in which individual needs could be met, a situation which was seen to offer emotional security as well as a stable learning environment. The provision of appropriate resource materials and the management of learning by specially trained staff who were sympathetic to the individual needs of slow learners were other advantages of this system, one in which pupils were seen to be 'protected from too much exposure to academic failure'. Some heads maintained that pupils' motivation increased in the sheltered academic environment of a special class while others reported that as slow learners worked through a carefully structured basic skills programme they also gained in self-confidence, both valuable spin-offs in terms of social adjustment. In many cases slow learners in a special class were taught by one member of staff for much of their academic timetable, i.e. for up to 40 per cent of the week. This was perceived to foster a feeling of security among slow learners and also provided the opportunity for one teacher to get to know each pupil very well indeed.

Most of the heads who organized special classes did so for the 11+ to 13+ age range only, stressing that the system eased what was often a difficult transition for children to make from junior to secondary school. The special class gave slow learners 'the opportunity to adapt to a new environment without too many changes' reported the head of a large (1650) urban comprehensive in the east midlands, which received pupils from five much smaller feeder schools each autumn.

The provision of a special but restricted curriculum for slow learners was commented on as a disadvantage by a number of head teachers. Where pupils had not studied certain subjects (most commonly a foreign language and a science) in the early years of secondary education, there was little opportunity for them to pick these up at a later date. Some heads recognized this as a problem for both late developers and for slow learners who were ready to join the mainstream after a period spent in a special class. More than one head stated with concern that such 'curriculum distancing' could result in choices at 4th and 5th year level being restricted for many slow learners who had previously followed a special curriculum in a special class.

Heads recognized that slow learners could feel isolated in separate classes and might be labelled as members of a special group with deleterious effects on pupils' self-confidence. Many noted with regret the few opportunities some slow learners had to mix with others in their year group. Other problems centred on reintegration and the difficulties experienced by slow learners when they left the special class and joined the mainstream. Many pupils, it was felt, had difficulty in 'keeping up' with the rest of the group and took time to adjust to frequent room changes and to meeting a number of subject specialists during the week, in contrast to the home room and class teacher situation to which many were accustomed.

A few head teachers were concerned that the special class system effectively established a limit, in terms of staffing and accommodation, on the numbers of slow learners for which a school could cater. This is explored more fully in Chapter three. Concerning identification, some heads pointed out that slow learners might be 'poor in one subject but not necessarily in all', hence the curricular limitations of a special class could be inappropriate. Others commented that, in a special class, initial misplacement of slow learners was a particular concern as problems of readjustment and reintegration were particularly difficult to resolve.

Slow Learner Sets

Slow learner sets, organized in 575 schools, were present in four-fifths of middle schools and in over three-fifths of other secondary schools. In only 18 schools were sets the only form of special provision made for slow learning pupils. Slow learner sets were provided for first year pupils in 40 per cent of the schools in the sample and were available for 4th and 5th year students in as many as 60 per cent of the schools. Sets were organized in every year and were found in year groups where mixed ability, bands, streams or sets were the dominant type of teaching unit. Separate slow learner sets were commonly organized for English and maths teaching but were less frequently provided for humanities, modern languages and science. In only a few schools were special sets established for slow learners taking craft and technical subjects in the 4th and 5th years.

In any year, sets were seen to offer the opportunity for slow learners to be taught by subject specialists in a smaller than usual group. Heads felt that this was an advantage since groups of up to 20 were small enough for pupils to receive a considerable amount of individual attention while at the same time avoiding the 'labelling' so often associated with a special class. Others commented on the fact that in sets slow learners were freed from the curricular restrictions experienced by members of a special class, that they were kept in the mainstream where they benefited from contact with pupils from a wider ability range and that, by receiving 'the complete range of opportunities', they were both socially and academically part of the community. Several heads stressed the importance of providing small sets in which pupils could progress 'at their own level and pace of work' in the care of specialist remedial teachers until they were deemed ready to join a mainstream group in those subjects in which they were reasonably able. It was felt that such a system was flexible enough to allow for the different rates at which pupils made progress and to cater well for late developers, as allowance was made for different subject abilities. Heads also emphasized the flexibility created by providing a slow learner set within the school's setting system, as pupils could easily move between sets as progress was made. 'Integration is the keynote' wrote one head whose opinion is typical of many who provided sets for slow learning pupils.

In a small number of schools, heads indicated that remedial staff acted as 'support' or 'floating' teachers in English, maths and social studies sets, assisting subject specialists by working with pupils who needed extra on-the-spot help in the classroom. The provision of this support would do much to solve the only problem heads identified in a setting system, namely that not all subject staff who taught slow learner sets knew what to expect of these pupils. For while English and many of the special maths sets were taught by remedial staff, slow learner sets in the sciences, humanities, craft, modern language and technical subjects were usually taught by subject specialists, few of whom had received any special training for this aspect of their work.

Options for Slow Learners

Fifty-three per cent of secondary schools provided slow learner options in years 4 and 5, where they were part of the option system organized across most of the curriculum for all pupils. In contrast, less than eight per cent of the sample provided special options for slow learners in the lower school, where these usually consisted of choices made within modern languages, science or craft subjects. Some slow learner options, with similar choices, were available in 11 per cent of middle schools.

Slow learner options consisted of specially designed courses which were sometimes taught by remedial staff but more usually by subject specialists. The provision of special options was seen to offer the slow learner 'parity of esteem with his peers', as all pupils were involved with making some kind of subject choice at the same time in their school career. One head saw the ability to choose optional subjects instead of being directed as a strength of this system, since, as he explained, 'the activity of choosing is an educational process in itself'. However, it was emphasized by many head teachers that pupils' choices for 4th and 5th year subjects were guided in order to reflect their 'career aspirations, external examination entry possibilities and general educational requirements'. In a number of schools, sets were used within the option system to provide for slow learners without segregating them from the mainstream; for example European studies could be taken as an alternative to a foreign language and rural studies instead of a 4th or 5th year pure science course. One head, who had recently switched from special classes to sets and options, reported that the new system had resulted in a considerable reduction in behaviour problems among slow learners in the upper school.

Many non-examination courses were available as options to 4th and 5th year pupils together with numbers of Mode III CSE courses which had been specially designed to meet the needs of pupils at the lower end of the ability range. Such options were available in every area of the curriculum; examples included money management, music appreciation, reading for pleasure, contemporary studies, child development, motor-cycle maintenance, science in society, home management, art and outdoor pursuits. In addition, some schools provided a 'support option' during which time slow learners could receive help from remedial specialists on any aspect of their course work. This enabled some pupils to study one subject less than the usual number and at the same time to receive extra help in any area of the curriculum as required. In a number of cases, a school-based leaving certificate was available to candidates who successfully completed a prescribed course of study which did not lead to an external examination, although it should be remembered that all schools offered non-examination work to slow learners as well as the opportunity for them to take CSE subjects if they wished.

The few disadvantages identified were concerned with the fact that slow learners in many schools had fewer 'real' option choices to make at 4th and 5th year level than did other pupils. This was partly seen to be the outcome of a restriction in the curriculum in the lower school and partly the result of a shortage of resources and of staff, which reduced the number of Mode III and non-examination courses which schools were able to offer. Some head teachers reported that by following special options slow learners still had limited contact with the rest of their year group.

A Withdrawal System

Pupils were withdrawn from their usual teaching groups in order to receive specialist remedial help in 85 per cent of the schools surveyed, making this the most widely used form of provision for slow learners in both middle and other secondary schools.

Withdrawal, which was observed to take place from slow learner classes as well as from every type of mainstream group, was regarded by many heads as a way of offering slow learners help with specific difficulties while at the same time avoiding 'labelling' and segregating them from their peers. In most schools a withdrawal system existed together with one or more other forms of provision for slow learners; in only 67 schools was it the only form of special teaching in all year groups up to and including the 5th year. Seventy-five per cent of schools made a withdrawal facility available to first and second year pupils, 68 per cent offered this to pupils in the third year (13+), 46 per cent withdrew pupils in the 4th year and 40 per cent withdrew 5th year pupils for special teaching.

Irrespective of whether the withdrawal system operated in the lower school only or in every year, heads cited similar advantages and disadvantages associated with this type of provision. Many commented on the fact that by sharing the same curriculum slow learners were given the same opportunities as others during early adolescence and were both socially and academically integrated into the school as a result. This strategy was observed to have a valuable spin-off in terms of boosting the self-confidence of those pupils who were less able in basic skills but who could achieve a measure of success in other areas of the curriculum, such as art, craft, design, music or PE. A number of head teachers considered that a combination of the 'stimulus of the mainstream', in which slow learners were taught by subject specialists, plus the advantages of regular individual tuition from skilled remedial staff resulted in 'better motivated' pupils, and were therefore wholeheartedly supportive of a withdrawal system in preference to any other. The head of one such school, in which pupils were withdrawn for individual help with reading, explained that, 'this improves self-esteem, motivation and gives them the opportunity to progress to the limit of their ability'. It was widely felt that by giving slow learners extra support in the basic 'tools of learning', by withdrawing them from the mainstream for only short periods of time, pupils were equipped in the best possible way to cope with normal teaching situations.

The importance to slow learners of maintaining peer-group friendships was stressed by many heads who saw a system of withdrawal as a way of ensuring that these associations were not broken. Slow learners could remain in their normal teaching or tutor groups and be withdrawn for extra help as and when this was deemed necessary. The flexibility of such a system, in which any pupil could receive help at any time and could be returned to the mainstream when sufficient progress had been made, was seen to be a particular strength of withdrawal and was cited by many as an advantage to both pupils and teachers. Several heads stated that by the third year of secondary education many slow learners had become fully integrated and no longer required extra support.

Heads also welcomed the opportunity afforded by withdrawal to use specialist remedial staff for individual diagnostic testing and evaluation, where this was most needed. In some schools remedial staff joined mainstream classes to help with the early identification and diagnosis of learning difficulties among new entrants, while in others they worked beside subject specialists to help any pupils with problems and to support and monitor the progress of slow learners who had recently rejoined the group.

A number of schools supplemented their withdrawal programme by using volunteer parents or 6th form students to hear pupils read or to help them complete simple written exercises for a specified time each week. Volunteers were guided and supervised by remedial staff and regular liaison took place to check on the individual problems and progress of each pupil. This scheme had the great advantage of extending the amount of individual tuition time for the slow learner each week, without extending the teaching load of the remedial staff by the same amount. Also, as several heads pointed out, by withdrawing pupils for help as this was needed, the establishment of an 'over-protected' group or, worse, a 'sink' group of slow learners was avoided.

While some head teachers detected no disadvantages in the system, others pointed out that pupils who had missed lessons as a consequence of being withdrawn for coaching were frequently faced with the problem of catching up missed work in their own time. To try to overcome this problem, staff in some schools organized withdrawal for basic skills coaching during English and maths time, so the lesson was an alternative rather than an extra one; others provided tuition in basic skills for slow learners instead of French so that they took no foreign language but received additional help in literacy – a less flexible arrangement because of the effects of a restricted curriculum, but one which was seen to reduce the pressure on slow learning pupils. However, in the majority of schools, pupils were left to make up missed work in their own time and the head who wrote of this, 'On balance we think the benefits outweigh the disadvantages', expressed the views of many on the same issue.

Other disadvantages mentioned included the comment that a few pupils initially experienced a certain amount of embarrassment at being pointed out as a 'slow learner' who had to leave the class periodically to receive extra help and the observation that some slow learners did not respond well to working on their own in mainstream groups. Even in the 4th and 5th years some were seen to lack confidence and to give up easily. A few heads noted that many of those pupils who suffered a loss of motivation, rapidly became bored and disruptive unless measures were taken to ensure their involvement in the lesson. While it was acknowledged that teachers in certain curricular areas experienced this problem more frequently than others, difficulties associated with the pace of work, with homework tasks and with teacher expectation generally were all recorded.

In summary, it appears that pupils were withdrawn from a particular teaching group for one of three reasons. In some schools slow learners left a special class to obtain extra help with specific difficulties, while in others pupils were withdrawn from the mainstream for individual or small group coaching by remedial department staff. In a few schools slow learners were withdrawn from a special class and attached to a mainstream group on a subject by subject basis until integration was complete, or as complete as was considered desirable. 'Integration is available and is used when the pupil is ready', wrote one head, who saw this system as a most satisfactory way of providing for the changing needs of slow learners.

2.4 An Appraisal of the Most Widely Used Methods of Organizing Provision for Slow Learners

As Table 2.1 shows, 22 per cent of schools in the sample used a combination of special classes, sets, options and withdrawal in providing for the needs of slow learners, 16 per cent employed both sets and withdrawal and 13 per cent adopted sets, options and withdrawal as a means of organizing special or supplementary teaching for slow learning pupils. Examples drawn from these three groups, which together constitute over half of the schools surveyed, are used in the paragraphs which follow to illustrate how different strategies may be combined to make provision for slow learners.

Slow Learner Classes, Sets and Options

The largest group comprised the 24 per cent of secondary and eight per cent of middle schools in which provision was made by means of special classes, sets and options together with a withdrawal facility. In 23 of these 176 schools, additional help was also made available. In some schools 'floating' remedial specialists joined certain lower school mainstream classes to help pupils who had learning difficulties, while, in others, 6th form students and volunteer parents heard pupils read on a one-to-one basis. A peripatetic teacher for slow learners with additional severe language difficulties regularly visited one school and in another slow learners for whom English was a second language attended a nearby language centre each week to receive extra help. Thus the efforts of this subgroup of schools to provide a purposeful and comprehensive programme of special provision for slow learners whose problems were so varied resulted in departmental remedial work and subject-specific support as well as the use of outside help from individuals and institutions.

In all of the schools, whether or not outside agents were used, the four kinds of pupil groups were combined in a great variety of ways, resulting in many different systems of provision for slow learners. However, classes, sets and withdrawal were all widely used in years 1 to 3, while special options dominated the 4th and 5th years, frequently augmented by setting and in many cases supported by withdrawal.

Only 12 schools offered all four kinds of special provision to every year group and it should be noted that seven of these had intakes aged 13+ and 14+. Thus it was rare for classes, sets, options and withdrawal to be available in every year from 1 to 5. One school in which this was the case organized a special class in year 1 after a settling in period of two to three weeks, during which time decisions on allocation to this group were made. Its members, however, remained in mixed ability tutor groups for registration. Slow learner sets were established for English, maths and modern language studies while special courses for slow learners were provided within the craft options and also by the science and environmental studies departments. Pupils were guided towards a range of 4th and 5th year options in which the emphasis was placed on basic skills and craft subjects, and it was usual for slow learners in this school to take CSE Mode III examinations in the 5th year. Slow learners could be withdrawn for extra help in any year.

Some schools in this group, i.e. in which all four methods of organization for slow learner provision were employed, chose to register the pupils in the special class separately from others in their year group. Several schools also made provision for 6th form students with learning difficulties to take extra English classes, designed mainly, but not exclusively, for pupils for whom English was a second language. In one-fifth of these 176 schools, provision of one kind was restricted to particular year groups. One such school organized a small class in the first year, where pupils followed a special curriculum which did not include modern languages. As the head explained:

This class provides a secure base at the changeover from primary to secondary education when many slow learners feel insecure. It gives the teacher a chance to get to know the pupils very well indeed and to better understand their difficulties. In years 2 and 3 slow learners are withdrawn from French. This ensures that progress (in literacy) is maintained but at the same time allows pupils to mix fully with others.

In the second and third years a special maths set was also established to cater for slow learners who joined other pupils in bands and sets for the rest of the curriculum. In the 4th and 5th years, all pupils were catered for by the school's option and setting system within which slow learners followed a special Combined Studies course for half of their timetable. After consultation between parents, pupils and staff a number of slow learning pupils followed special mainstream option courses and it was customary for some to take CSE Mode I and Mode III examinations in the 5th year. While the head was aware that slow learners missed the opportunity to study a foreign language, this was the only difficulty identified within this pattern of special provision.

The final example illustrates a different way of using a special class. In this school slow learners were withdrawn to receive special help during years 1 and 2 and a special class was organized in the third year, while options and sets dominated in the 4th and 5th. Special sets were organized in all years for English and maths. The head acknowledged that some slow learners experienced difficulties in mainstream classes but this he felt was minimized in the streamed situation prevailing in years 1 to 3. Thus in contrast to example two, where the special class was deemed particularly helpful for new entrants, in this school a slow learner class was not organized until the third year, the head preferring to cater for pupils' needs in mainstream sets and streams supplemented by withdrawal for the first two years of their secondary education.

Sets plus Withdrawal

The second most widely used system of slow learner provision involved the organization of special sets and a withdrawal facility. This was the system adopted by almost half of the middle schools and by rather more than one-tenth of other secondary schools. In all, 16 per cent of the sample made provision for slow learners in this way, supplemented in some cases by mainstream support from 'floating teachers' and special resources, and by peripatetic teachers, volunteer parents and 6th form helpers.

The particular strengths of setting and withdrawal lay in their flexibility to cater for the different and differing needs of slow learning pupils. An example was provided by one junior high school in which pupils were registered and taught in mixed ability groups for all subjects except maths. Remedial department staff identified pupils who were in need of additional help. Some, after diagnostic testing, were withdrawn from all mainstream English lessons and provided with an alternative learning programme. Others, whose problems were less severe, were withdrawn from two or three English lessons per week to be given support in areas of specific weakness. Maths was taught in sets, with a small slow learner set identified by the maths department following a separate course taught by a remedial specialist. Slow learners receiving literacy help did not necessarily join the numeracy set, and vice versa.

Throughout the school it was the policy to integrate slow learners as fully as possible and to this end a programme of in-class support in English, maths, science and humanities had been offered for a number of years, with considerable success. At the time of the research, this programme had been curtailed because of staffing reductions, but remedial teachers were still able to offer support in humanities and science in the form of resource design and production and as 'floating' teachers in some lessons, helping those pupils who were experiencing problems. Additional help was available during the lunch hour and before school for pupils of all abilities who needed help with handwriting or with spelling.

In this group of schools, it was common to find both sets and withdrawal available in the same year; in only nine schools were the two forms of special provision offered to different year groups. An example was provided by one school in which slow learners were withdrawn from mainstream mixed ability classes in the first year and taught in special sets for humanities, maths and French studies in subsequent years. The school organized bands and sets for all classes in years 2 to 5 and the head felt that this system gave slow learners the best possible opportunity to integrate, to receive specialist teaching and to follow the same school curriculum as other pupils.

Sets, Options and Withdrawal

Thirteen per cent of schools in the sample employed sets, special options and a withdrawal system in order to cater for the needs of slow learners. As shown in Table 2.1, only three of these were middle schools, where pupils aged 11+ were offered both options and withdrawal in addition to sets, but it was extremely rare for three kinds of special provision to be offered to one year group in other secondary schools. In most, withdrawal was available from the entry year, together with slow learner sets for some or all of the major academic subjects. In approximately half of the secondary schools this withdrawal facility extended to the fifth year and in half it ceased after the third year. Special option courses for slow learners were generally made available in the upper school; only one secondary school in 14 arranged slow learner options in any of years 1 to 3.

A typical example of a system of sets, options and withdrawal was provided by one school in which the head of lower school placed all pupils in mixed ability groups for their first year, during the course of which setting was introduced in maths and modern languages. Pupils in need of additional help by withdrawal were identified from information contained in primary records and supplemented by results from a *Daniels and Diack Test 12* (Test of Reading Experience) administered during the early weeks of the autumn term. During modern language lessons pupils took French, European studies or spent this time in the extra studies department where they received support in literacy and language skills. In the upper school, slow learners were guided by the staff in consultation with parents over their choice of options. In addition to maths, which was set, English, which was taught in bands, and careers, RE and social education, all of which were taught in mixed ability groups, slow learners were offered specially designed option courses in technical science, extra English and integrated craft. The head felt that this system was particularly helpful in providing for slow learners' needs. He wrote:

> In many cases pupils derive confidence and make progress in a small-group withdrawal situation and are able to return to full-time mainstream classes within three years. When this is not possible it is feasible for pupils to receive extra tuition in basic skills as an option course in the upper school. The scheme has worked well and is socially advantageous as pupils are able to mix fully with their peers.

Sixth Form Provision

There were 117 schools in which special arrangements were made for 6th form pupils with learning difficulties, representing 26 per cent of those with 6th form students. This provision included spelling and handwriting groups, extra English classes, the withdrawal of pupils for whom English was a second language to form a special group or to attend a language centre, link courses with local colleges of further education, the use of peripatetic ESL staff for Chinese and Asian pupils, the inclusion of remedial department staff in the 6th form General Studies team and numerous instances of individual coaching sessions in reading, English, spelling and handwriting. In some schools, 6th form students were given the opportunity to decide whether or not they wished to receive specialist help from remedial staff, and individual remedial tuition was offered on a voluntary basis. A few schools provided special courses for 6th formers with learning difficulties; for example, one had established a group which was working towards CSE English and another was piloting a basic clerical procedures course, in conjunction with the local FE college.

2.5 Discussion

The question of how best to provide for the needs of slow learners is in no way resolved by the examples quoted here. What this chapter has done is to highlight the strengths of specific modes of organization in catering for slow learners and point out their weaknesses as perceived by head teachers who have had the opportunity to see and to note the outcomes of a given system over a period of time and are therefore in a position to make an evaluation of its success in terms of the school's aims and policy for slow learning pupils.

There is, understandably, considerable consensus over the benefits which accrue from certain modes of organization in the education of slow learners as well as the problems which these can generate. Widely held beliefs about the stable, secure learning environment provided by a small, special class, taught for most of the time by one remedial teacher, have led to its adoption by many schools for pupils in the early years of their secondary education. It was found that special classes were organized in schools in which the mainstream grouping was predominantly mixed ability as well as in those where sets, bands or streams were common. In the upper school, special classes existed in almost one-quarter of the schools sampled, in systems which were predominantly a mixture of options and sets.

A slow learner set was seen to offer the added advantage to those cited above, of flexibility, as slow learners could be catered for in special sets or in mainstream sets according to need and had the opportunity to move 'up' or 'down' within subject sets. The generally small size of slow learner sets in which specialist teaching was available was seen to provide a particularly helpful learning environment for these pupils. It was common for those schools in which sets were organized from entry until the 5th year to offer special English and maths sets throughout, whether the dominant form of pupil grouping was mixed ability, bands, sets or streams. Thus the benefits to slow learners of special sets in the early secondary years were more frequently seen to be in the support given in basic skills. In the upper school, where sets were a common form of whole school organization, special groups for slow learners were established in other subjects also, with some CSE courses available.

Slow learners in the upper school frequently took a selection of options, some of which were setted, as well as a core of basic subjects. Where special options were offered, as they were in over half of the schools (356/678), these covered a wide range of subjects, reflecting the school's aims which were to provide a preparation for adult life and to give slow learners the opportunity of mixing with other pupils in their year group. The topics covered were diverse and the emphasis was clearly on situations which pupils were likely to experience on leaving school, since in most cases basic skills were offered alongside these options in small classes, sets or withdrawal groups. Options for slow learners offered some opportunity for choice and enabled all pupils to participate in the same option system.

Withdrawal was the method most widely used to provide support for slow learners. Over half of the schools adopted this method of organization in the first three years and one-third in the 4th and 5th years. In most cases withdrawal operated in conjunction with one or more of the other systems of special provision, offering extra help in basic skills for those who required it. Pupils were withdrawn from mixed ability, banded, setted and streamed groups to receive extra help, and although it was acknowledged that a few of them experienced problems on rejoining the mainstream again, the consensus of opinion among heads was that the benefits of near full-time integration with the mainstream outweighed the difficulties pupils encountered on rejoining the group after a period of special help elsewhere.

Head teachers were shown to be sensitive to the changing needs of slow learners at different stages of their educational development and were aware of both shortcomings and benefits in the special provision made within their schools. The many different ways in which classes, sets, options and withdrawal were combined were indicative of a widespread concern over the welfare of slow learners, as heads attempted, within the constraints of existing building space, timetable and staffing ratios, to make appropriate provision for their needs.

The long-term outcomes of specific modes of special provision cannot be measured in this study but must await further research. However, it was apparent from head teachers' comments that the kind of provision offered was constantly under review and hence likely to change from one school year to the next.

The head of a newly established 11–16 comprehensive explained:

> The whole dilemma over 'which system' seems dependent upon the number of pupils in need of extra help. We attempt to help quite a number spreading our help thinly. Would we be better to help in more depth?

Another reported that:

> We adapt our provision in small ways each year to suit each new group, and also to make full use of staff strengths.

Further up the school frequent revision took place, as exemplified by this head who wrote:

> We have constantly to examine our courses at 4th and 5th year level to ensure that courses of a suitable kind are operating for slow learners.

Beside these accounts of annual changes made and those planned were many comments indicating that heads wished to extend the remedial help presently available. As Chapter three will indicate, not all pupils with low reading ages were found to be receiving special help and heads saw an increase in the staffing establishment as one means of meeting the needs of these pupils. While a few simply wanted 'more generous staffing', most were quite specific about the areas of greatest need and how such staff should be deployed. 'Greater use of withdrawal', 'a remedial specialist working in major subject areas to advise on syllabus and approaches', 'an extra teacher for remedial maths' were all comments frequently made. 'An increase in staffing provision to reduce group size and to extend individual teaching higher up the ability range' was seen as a priority by many heads while others wanted 'sufficient staff time to inject a second teacher to help in specialist departments'. A number of heads wanted to use an increased remedial staff allocation to develop and run special courses for slow learners in the 4th and 5th years, and several mentioned the desirability of structuring an integrated programme for this age group.

The contents of this chapter have shown that the provision made for slow learners in secondary schools is extremely varied in type and in compass. Different forms of pupil grouping, perceived to have specific benefits, have been explored in their proper educational context, i.e. with regard to other forms of teaching unit present in the schools in question. While head teachers and their staff can offer an evaluation based on observation and experience, even this should be interpreted with caution, for it does not follow that any given system will necessarily have the same pay-offs in another school. Differences in catchment area, timetabling and staffing can be crucial. Head teachers, aware of these changing factors, revealed that provision for slow learners was under constant review as they attempted to match perceived needs with available resources. Some felt that they were catering for all those pupils who required extra help; others considered that the provision made was inadequate in view of the nature and extent of the difficulties identified, and saw a partial solution in the allocation of more trained staff.

Chapter three

The Identification of Slow Learners

Pupils with special needs are apt to suffer most at the transition stages in their education unless systematic arrangements are made to ensure their needs are known and essential information is available at each stage to those who need it. (Education Survey 15, 1971)

3.1 Introduction

In this chapter the procedures used to allocate all pupils to teaching groups are outlined, and an account of transition arrangements in three schools with contrasting systems illustrates the implications of these different systems for slow learners.

The questionnaire survey revealed that in identifying slow learners, teachers relied heavily on the results from a variety of reading tests. The project team therefore sought a common measure which could be used to assess the reading ages of pupils in all case study schools. In the second half of the chapter, results from the reading test which was selected for this purpose are examined in the light of information on the pupils for whom slow learner provision was made in each school.

3.2 Liaison with Feeder Schools

Each year secondary school heads are faced with the task of providing continuity of educational experience for a new intake which includes pupils from a wide range of ability and who come from a variety of different educational backgrounds. The questionnaire survey revealed that 48 per cent of secondary schools in the sample received pupils from more than ten feeder schools each autumn (Table 3.1) and one in three of these received pupils from more than 20 feeders. Comments from the staff indicated that interpreting and utilizing information from such varied sources presented problems for those involved with the placement of pupils into teaching or tutor groups.

Table 3.1: *Secondary schools and contributory feeder schools: size of secondary school and number of feeder schools† (N=672).*

No. of Feeder Schools	<250	251–500	501–750	751–1000	1001–1250	1251–1500	1501–1750	>1751	Total Schools	%
1– 5	4	23	27	33	23	14	8	–	132	(20)
6–10	3	18	50	59	53	27	8	–	218	(32)
11–15	–	12	31	44	28	13	6	4	138	(21)
16–20	–	4	18	16	17	7	4	2	68	(10)
21–25	–	1	13	12	12	5	3	–	46	(7)
Over 25	–	3	13	21	17	8	6	2	70	(10)
	7	61	152	185	150	74	35	8	672	(100)

No response – 26 schools
† The 93 middle schools are excluded from this table.

Several factors contributed to the existence of very large numbers of feeder schools supplying pupils to one secondary school. Many inner city schools, single sex schools and church schools were found to have large numbers of contributory feeders. Examples included a mixed school of 1750 pupils, located in a metropolitan area to which new entrants from over 50 primary schools were admitted, a church school with a roll of 955 which took pupils from 32 feeder primaries and a boys' comprehensive of 740 which received a few pupils from each of 40 feeder schools.

Information from Feeder Schools

In 95 per cent of secondary schools in the survey, staff used information from feeder schools in order to allocate pupils to teaching groups. Table 3.2 shows the nature of the information provided and it is evident that secondary schools received many different combinations of these items from the primary or middle feeder schools from which their new entrants were drawn.

Table 3.2: *Information obtained before entry to secondary schools and used for the allocation of all pupils to teaching groups.* $(N=658)†$

Items Used	Schools Receiving Information	
	N	%
Reading age	394	(60)
Verbal reasoning score	312	(47)
Non-verbal reasoning score	159	(24)
Standardized English attainment test score	235	(36)
Standardized maths attainment test score	252	(38)
General attainment grade	204	(31)
Marks from school tests/examinations	112	(17)
Teachers' comments on attainment	462	(70)
Teachers' comments on attitude to school/ personal qualities	399	(61)
Friendships	282	(43)
Other – eg. spelling age, foreign language ability, parents' wishes, musical ability, ethnic group, Welsh language proficiency	208	(32)

† 40 schools did not use information received from feeder schools.

A problem was created by the use of different tests, as the reading ages, verbal and non-verbal reasoning scores, English and maths results provided by feeder schools could have been obtained from one of a number of different published tests, many of which examined different sub-skills and were thus not strictly comparable.

Problems also arose because of the diversity of standards in the feeder primary or middle schools, as school-devised tests and examinations, general attainment grades and teachers' comments on attitude were all relative to the ability range and teacher expectations within individual feeder schools. Records of this sort were therefore not comparable either. The problems of teachers' assessments were exemplified by the head of lower school in a large comprehensive who asked heads to categorize pupils as below average/average/above average but found that standards varied considerably between the 16 feeder schools, making interpretation of assessments difficult, and that results from small schools were particularly unreliable.

Some local education authorities were attempting to overcome such problems by developing test programmes in the feeder schools. In one LEA, the *Neale Reading Test* was used by all primary schools; in another, the *London Reading Test* was administered and the results used to allocate a balanced intake to each secondary school. Some secondary schools had devised programmes of testing for use in their feeder schools; for example one received the results of the NFER verbal reasoning, comprehension, English and maths tests for all new entrants. In some areas however there was resistance to a common testing programme in feeder schools as this was felt to be a 'retrograde step which could be viewed as an underhand way of perpetuating the 11+' and staff in one school reported that standardized test results were no longer available from any of the feeder schools in their LEA.

3.3 The Allocation of Pupils to Teaching Groups

Only 26 per cent (182/698) of secondary schools in the survey reported that the head of the remedial department or teacher with responsibility for slow learners was officially involved in the allocation of slow learners to teaching groups. In almost half of these schools the remedial teacher was one of a team and, as in the majority of schools, allocation to teaching groups was the responsibility of one or more of the senior management staff, i.e. head, deputy head, head of lower school or head of year. Teams occasionally included subject department heads, class teachers, curriculum co-ordinators, school counsellors, liaison teachers, heads of house and educational psychologists.

In a few schools, the head of the remedial department was consulted informally concerning the placement of pupils who were considered by feeder school staff to be 'slow learners', but in many schools there was no consultation. As one head of a remedial department commented, 'We are presented with pupils for our classes by the appropriate head of year and therefore can only test and make comments and recommendations after the 'fait accompli!'

Timing of Allocation Procedures

Decisions concerning the placement of pupils in teaching groups were made before entry in 55 per cent of the 698 secondary schools. In another 32 per cent of schools, allocation was arranged before entry and adjustments made after initial tests or after observation and testing during a diagnostic period. In the remaining 13 per cent of schools pupils were allocated to teaching groups after a settling in or diagnostic period which varied from one week in some schools to a year in others.

In order to place pupils in teaching groups, staff in all but five per cent of the schools used information provided by feeder schools. However in about half of the schools in the sample this was supplemented with information obtained after entry. Table 3.2 shows the nature of the information received before entry and Table 3.3 shows the information obtained after pupils' entry to secondary school.

Table 3.3: *Information obtained after entry to secondary school and used for allocation to teaching groups. (N=360)†*

Items Used	Number of Schools Using Items	
	N	%
Reading age	208	(58)
Verbal reasoning score	76	(21)
Non-verbal reasoning score	73	(20)
Standardized English attainment test score	117	(33)
Standardized maths attainment test score	131	(36)
General attainment grade	46	(13)
Marks from school tests/examinations	145	(40)
Teachers' comments on attainment	153	(43)
Teachers' comments on attitude to school/ personal qualities	91	(25)
Friendships	20	(6)
Other – eg. spelling age, results of dictation test, assessment of specific needs, information from psychologists' reports, results of testing by remedial staff	65	(18)

† 338 schools did not use information obtained after entry.

The most commonly used criteria for allocating pupils to teaching groups were the reading ages and comments on attainment, attitude to school and personal qualities which were received from feeder schools. Friendship ties and the results of standardized English or maths tests provided by primary school teachers were often taken into consideration also (Table 3.2). In some schools, information from feeder schools was supplemented by the heads of remedial departments or teachers with responsibility for slow learners who visited primary and middle schools during the summer term preceding entry in order to gather more details about pupils who would possibly be placed in their care.

Reading ages obtained after entry were used in 30 per cent of all secondary schools in the survey as a check to ensure that pupils had been placed in appropriate teaching groups. Other information commonly obtained after entry and used similarly included the results from standardized maths and English tests, school examination results and teachers' comments on attainment. (Table 3.3.)

Information from feeder schools was used to group pupils in different ways, depending upon the organization of the school and the policy for slow learner provision. As Table 3.4 shows, on entry to

Table 3.4: *Type of teaching group to which pupils were allocated on entry to secondary school. (N=698)*

	Mixed Ability	Band	Stream	Set	Option	None Dominant	Total
11+	309	124	67	30	0	49	579
12+	15	14	5	5	0	9	48
13+	13	15	2	6	0	13	49
14+	0	1	0	1	4	4	10
	337	154	74	42	4	75	686

No response – 12 schools.

secondary school at the age of 11+, 12+, 13+ or 14+ pupils could be allocated to mixed ability teaching groups, bands, streams, sets or special classes. In 49 per cent of secondary schools new entrants were allocated to mixed ability groups, but one in three of these schools also organized a separate small special class for the slowest pupils in the intake. In 22 per cent of secondary schools the information received before entry was used to place pupils in groups, each of which represented one section of the ability range. The least able were placed in the bottom band, within which teaching groups could be mixed in ability or streamed, and it was common for one or more of these classes to become the special slow learner class. Approximately one in four of these schools used test results or teachers' assessments obtained after entry in order to make adjustments to the bands, mainly during the first half of the autumn term. Streams were the predominant teaching unit for new entrants in 11 per cent of the secondary schools surveyed. In 68 of these 74 schools, pupils were placed in streamed classes on the basis of information received from primary schools. In two out of every three of these schools, teachers obtained further information after entry as a result of which some adjustments were made. In six schools, pupils were streamed shortly after entry on the basis of results from a variety of tests, including reading age, taken during the first few weeks of term.

In six per cent of secondary schools pupils were taught in sets during their first year. In half of these schools pupils were placed in sets using information received from primary schools alone and in half both primary records and information obtained after entry to secondary school were used. In 11 per cent of the secondary schools surveyed pupils joined different groups for different subjects and there was no dominant teaching unit in the entry year. The most commonly used groups in such schools were found to be sets and mixed ability classes.

3.4 Testing in Secondary Schools

In the majority of secondary schools in the survey, tests were used during the first year both to make adjustments to teaching groups and to ascertain the nature and extent of the problems of those pupils who were recorded as having learning difficulties. Testing programmes were usually organized by one of the senior management team or by the head of the remedial department or teacher responsible for slow learners. In some schools all new entrants were tested; in others only those allocated to the special class(es) or those referred by subject specialists. In order to learn more about how slow learners' needs were identified and diagnosed, the project team explored this issue in detail.

Testing of Slow Learners

A questionnaire was sent to 661 heads of slow learner departments and teachers in charge of slow learner provision in secondary and middle schools in order to establish which tests were most commonly used with these pupils. Teachers were asked to specify the purposes for which tests were used and replies from 50 middle and 397 other secondary schools indicated that a number of the same tests were widely used to identify slow learning pupils, to diagnose the nature of their learning difficulties and to monitor progress.

In the paragraphs which follow, details received from middle schools are excluded, since provision for slow learners after their transfer into the secondary sector is quite a different issue from the situation in middle schools where a pupil aged 11+ merely moves year group and does not transfer to another school.

In response to the questionnaire item, 397 heads of remedial department and teachers in charge of slow learner provision indicated which standardized tests and diagnostic instruments they used to identify slow learning pupils in the new intake. (Table 3.5).

Table 3.5: *Tests used to 'identify' slow learning pupils after entry to secondary school.* $(N = 327)$

	Number of Schools Using Test
Daniels and Diack Test 12	114
NFER Non Verbal Test DH	46
Schonell Silent Reading Tests R3 or R4	37
Neale Analysis of Reading Ability	33
Gap Reading Comprehension Test	32
Burt/Vernon Reading Test	31
Schonell R1 – Word Recognition Test	31
Holborn Reading Scale	25

Replies indicated that tests were used for this purpose in 82 per cent of the schools surveyed (327/397). Although 86 different tests were used, most of which tested reading or verbal ability, including spelling, a relatively small number were widely used. (A complete list appears in Appendix 3A.1.)

The Daniels and Diack Test 12, also known as the Graded Test of

Reading Experience, proved to be the test most widely used to identify slow learners. It is a group reading test of the sentence completion type and was first published in 1958. Test 12 is readily available, easy to administer and to score, and has the added advantage of being inexpensive as it can easily be typed and duplicated. It is also one of the few tests which discriminate at the lower ability levels. However, the disadvantages are that because it was originally published some 24 years ago the material contains certain words and concepts which are not as familiar to children today as they were in the 1950s, and although reading ages up to 14 years are given, 'reading ages above ten years are unreliable and misleading' (Daniels and Diack, 1958).

The second most widely used test was the *NFER Non Verbal Reasoning DH*. Designed for an age range of 10 to 15 years, the test was first constructed in 1951 but was restandardized for pupils aged 11.3 to 12.9 years in 1974. It comprises 96 non verbal items and tasks which involve matching shapes and sequencing. The test is comparatively inexpensive as the test booklets can be re-used, and pupils record answers on separate sheets. However, although the material is suitable for the age range it should be noted that Test DH 'gives a measure of non verbal reasoning ability. The results should not be taken to indicate capacity for learning' (NFER, 1981).

The Schonell Silent Reading Tests R3 and R4, used in 37 schools, were first published in 1942. They are now produced as re-usable booklets with separate pupil answer sheets. The format of the booklets is old fashioned and the language may appear unsophisticated to pupils today. For example, 'I have a cat. It is black and white. It is one year old. It sleeps in a box. It likes to play with a ball of wool. Where does the cat sleep?' (Oliver and Boyd, 1942). Norms are dated and no information is given concerning reliability and validity.

The *Neale Analysis of Reading Ability* was used in 33 of the 397 schools to identify slow learners. This diagnostic test, published in 1957 and constructed for pupils aged between six and 12, assesses accuracy, speed and comprehension in reading by means of individual oral tests. As it is designed to detect specific errors in reading it takes about 20 minutes per pupil to administer and for this reason is not recommended for the identification of large numbers of pupils with learning problems.

The *Gap Reading Comprehension Test* was used in 32 schools.

Published in 1970, the test is designed to assess the child's reading comprehension of continuous prose by the use of the cloze procedure, but Pumfrey (1976) has drawn attention to a lack of detail concerning the standardization and reliability of the test.

The *Burt Reading Test* and *Schonell Graded Word Test* are both oral word recognition tests which are of limited value as a means of identifying slow learners, particularly as both are commonly used in the primary schools, and consequently many children are already familiar with the content. The *Holborn Reading Scale*, first published in 1948, was reissued unaltered in 1980. The format lacks visual appeal and some of the sentences may be almost incomprehensible to the pupil. For example, 'These documents constitute an authoritative record of a unique colonial enterprise' (Harrap, 1980).

The choice of tests used to identify slow learners at the time of transition from the primary to the secondary sector is limited by the fact that there are very few up-to-date tests which are suitable for use with pupils of low ability in the 11+ age group. The most widely used well-known tests are inexpensive and/or easy to administer, but *Daniels and Diack Test 12*, *Schonell R3 and R4*, the *Burt* and *Schonell* word recognition tests, the *Holborn Reading Scale* and the *Neale Analysis of Reading Ability* are all over twenty years old. Four out of the eight tests − Burt, Schonell, Holborn and Neale − are time-consuming oral tests which are therefore not particularly suitable for use when large numbers of pupils are involved. It is doubtful whether any one of these tests used alone is an appropriate way of identifying slow learners in a school's intake year and it may be for this reason that staff in the majority of schools, 75 per cent, chose to use more than one test for identification purposes.

Where more than one test was used, this was sometimes an attempt to identify weaknesses in different areas; for example, the *Schonell Comprehension*, *Blackwell Spelling* and *Vernon Arithmetic* tests were used in one school and a combination of *Daniels and Diack Reading Experience*, *Burt Word Recognition*, *Blackwell Spelling*, *NFER Maths* and *NFER Non Verbal DH* tests in another. However in some schools as many as three different reading tests were used to identify slow learners. Examples include *Daniels and Diack Test 12*, the *Schonell* and *Burt Word Recognition Tests* used together, and a combination of the *Young Reading Test*, *Daniels and Diack Test 12* and the *Neale Analysis*.

In 70 per cent of the 397 secondary schools surveyed, tests were used to gain a profile of the individual capabilities of slow learners (Table 3.6). Teachers used 94 different tests or test batteries for this purpose, half of which were tests of reading or verbal ability, including spelling. Other published tests which formed parts of test batteries included tests of lateral dominance, Welsh language tests, behaviour scales and tests of auditory discrimination. (See Appendix 3A.2 for the complete list.)

Table 3.6: *Tests used to gain a profile of the individual capabilities of slow learners. (N = 277)*

	Number of Schools Using Test
Daniels and Diack (Tests 1–12)	121
Neale Analysis	69
Aston Index	57
Jackson Phonic Skills	30
Raven's Standard Matrices	27
Schonell Spelling	27
Schonell R1 – Graded Word	26

Daniels and Diack Tests, described earlier in the chapter, were again the most widely used. The whole diagnostic battery of tests 1–12 was used to gain a profile of the capabilities of the slow learners. The *Neale Analysis*, used in some schools for identification purposes, was used in others for gaining a profile of the slow learner. This test is designed to detect specific errors in reading. The *Aston Index*, used in 57 schools, is a battery of tests which claims to distinguish the particular problems of the child so that an appropriate teaching programme can be planned. Many of these tests are restricted psychological tests and are therefore not available to all remedial teachers. The *Jackson Phonic Skills Test*, used in 30 schools, consists of a battery of 11 tests which can be used as a checklist of skills mastered by the pupil. The test contains guidance on the interpretation of results and suggestions for developing individual remedial programmes and is intended for pupils aged between five and ten years. *Raven's Standard Matrices*, used in 27 schools, is a non verbal mental ability test containing five sets of diagrammatic problems, sometimes used in conjunction with the

Mill Hill Vocabulary Scale and intended for pupils aged between eight and 14 years. *Schonell* spelling tests were used in 27 schools and the *Schonell Graded Word Test* in 26. These tests, although published many years ago, were still popular with teachers, who found them an easy to use method of assessing reading and spelling. In 70 per cent of these 277 schools, teachers used more than one test or test battery to gain information on the capabilities of individual pupils.

Some heads of remedial departments were attempting to construct for themselves a battery of tests which would give a profile of the slow learner by combining standardized and school-based tests. One of these used school-produced comprehension, spelling and dictation tests and the *Burt Reading Test*, combining the results to give a basic literacy score. Another school used a battery of tests which investigated home background, physical and perceptual faculties, basic sight vocabulary and phonic skills. Clearly the compilation of such batteries requires considerable knowledge of test construction and of the contents of commercially produced tests; a great deal of time on the part of the teachers is called for as well as expertise in the interpretation of scores.

There were pupils in the care of remedial staff whose behavioural and emotional problems were entwined with their lack of progress in the classroom. Sixty-five of the 397 heads of remedial departments in secondary schools reported that they used some tests to investigate these problems, the most widespread being the *Bristol Social Adjustment Guide* which was used in 47 of these 65 schools. (A complete list appears in Appendix 3A.3.)

In 87 per cent of the schools (345/397) tests were used as a means of monitoring the reading progress of slow learners while in 41 per cent (164/397), tests were used to measure progress in other curricular areas, primarily maths and spelling.

3.5 Allocation and Identification Procedures in Three Schools

During the fieldwork stage of the project, procedures used to allocate all pupils to teaching groups and to identify and provide for slow learners at the time of transition were investigated. Three schools, each with a different type of predominant teaching unit for pupils in the intake year, are used to illustrate these procedures and to examine their implications for slow learners.

School A

This small urban school with 500 pupils on roll aged between 11 and 18 received new entrants from 14 feeder schools. Pupils were allocated to streams by the head of first year who used standardized English and maths test results from the feeder schools on which to base his decision making.

The first two or three weeks of the autumn term was a diagnostic or settling in period for new entrants, during which all pupils took a comprehension test and wrote an essay. Teachers were asked to observe the pupils and to comment on their attitudes and personal qualities. The head of the remedial department tested pupils in the fourth stream and any others who were referred to him by subject teachers, using the *Schonell Reading Test* and the *Daniels and Diack Test of Reading Experience Test 12*. At the time of the visit, *Schonell Reading Test* results from slow learners in the special 11+ first year class gave a range of reading ages from 6.0 to 8.9 years and *Daniels and Diack* a range of between 6.4 and 9.1 years.

School D

This urban school with just over 1000 pupils on roll aged between 11 and 16 accepted new entrants from nine feeder schools. While the predominant teaching unit was reported to be sets, pupils were in mixed ability groups for registration and for practical subjects. Pupils were allocated to teaching groups on entry, as all feeder schools supplied reading ages and general attainment grades plus comments from the teachers on attainment, personal qualities and on pupils' attitudes to school. The head of the remedial department, remedial staff and head of first year visited feeder schools to consult teachers about slow learning pupils and to administer the tests.

Using test results the head of first year and the head of the remedial department together made up the mixed ability registration groups, noting all those pupils who would probably need help from the remedial department. Test results and other information gained during visits to feeder schools were then used to place pupils in sets for English. Two first year English sets were taught by members of the remedial department. Maths sets were made up on the basis of test results from the feeder schools but a further test was given at the end of the first term in order to assess whether pupils were correctly placed. Social studies and science sets were derived by heads of subject departments on the recommendations of the head of first year and the head of the remedial department, with adjustments being made during the first term according to pupils' ability and aptitude. Other subjects such as art, craft and PE were taught in the mixed ability registration groups. There was no diagnostic or settling in period because continuous assessment took place in all subject departments. Pupils who had particular problems with literacy or numeracy were initially placed in the sets taught by remedial specialists for basic subjects. As individual problems were overcome so pupils were promoted to the next set.

Having first administered *Daniels and Diack Test 12*, with the aim of identifying pupils with learning difficulties, the head of the slow learner department then tested all pupils whom it was considered might need remedial help using *Raven's Matrices* and the *English Picture Vocabulary Tests*. Occasionally, the *Holborn Reading Scale* was used. Reading ages from *Daniels and Diack Test 12* in the remedial English set ranged from 6.1 to 10.3 years and in the borderline remedial set from 7.6 to 13.1 years, but of course test results were not the only criteria used when making decisions concerning the needs of the individual pupil. Detailed and comprehensive records were maintained by remedial staff; each pupil was viewed individually, weaknesses were diagnosed and appropriate measures taken to remedy problems.

School X

This was a large urban school with over 1750 pupils aged between 11 and 18 whose new entrants came from one major and 48 minor feeder schools. All first year pupils were taught in mixed ability classes to which they were allocated on entry. The team responsible for placing pupils, which included the deputy head, senior year tutors and the teacher with responsibility for primary liaison, visited feeder schools and gathered as much information as possible about the pupils. This included reading ages, verbal and non verbal reasoning quotients, English and maths test scores, general attainment grades, marks from school tests and examinations, teachers' comments on attainment, personal qualities and attitude to school, friendship patterns and medical and attendance records. Most weight was given to the reading age, verbal reasoning score and teachers' comments on attainment which were used to assist the placement of pupils in matched mixed ability groups. Arrangements were made for pupils known to have severe literacy problems to be withdrawn for extra help immediately.

After entry to the school all pupils were tested using *Young's Group Reading Test* and *Daniels and Diack Test 12*, a diagnostic dictation (*Peters*) and the *NFER AH4 Group Test of General Intelligence*. They were also given a handwriting test. From these results more pupils needing extra help were identified and arrangements were made by the head of the coaching department for these pupils to be withdrawn in very small groups of two or three, for remedial tuition. In order to diagnose individual weaknesses the head of the coaching department used *Daniels and Diack Test 1*. Records and samples of each pupil's work were kept by remedial staff so that individual programmes of work designed to remedy specific processes could be planned and progress monitored. At the time of our visit the 44 pupils receiving reading coaching recorded reading ages from 5.0 to 9.0 years on the *Daniels and Diack Test 12*. The results from *Young's Reading Test* showed a range of reading ages from 7.1 to 10.4 years. In addition to those who needed coaching in reading, 48 pupils were withdrawn for help with handwriting and 43 for assistance with spelling. The first year was considered to be a settling-in and diagnostic period for all pupils and changes to mixed ability groups were avoided.

3.6 Discussion

In each of the three schools, pupils were allocated to teaching groups before entry on the basis of information obtained as a result of liaison with the feeder schools. In school A, the information was used to separate pupils with the lowest scores from the mainstream for all subjects and remedial staff were responsible for this special slow learner class. In school D, the information was used to establish mixed ability groups for registration and for practical subjects and to place pupils in sets for maths, English, humanities and science. Remedial staff taught the lowest English and maths sets and a blocked timetable ensured that pupils could be moved between sets.

In school X, feeder school information was used to structure mixed ability classes from which remedial staff were able to withdraw slow learning pupils for help with literacy skills according to need.

As indicated earlier in the chapter the head of the remedial department was involved in allocating pupils to teaching groups in a minority of schools in the sample. For example, in school A, the head of department worked only with pupils who were placed by the head of year into the special class. In school X, however, it was not necessary for the head of the remedial department to be involved in allocation since slow learners were identified after entry and individual withdrawal provision made independently of the teaching groups.

The diagnostic period was also used for different purposes in the three schools. In school A, pupils were tested and observed and at the end of two or three weeks adjustments were made if it appeared that a pupil had been misplaced. Any movement meant a major change of teaching group for the pupil. In school D, diagnosis was part of the policy of continuous assessment which aimed to ensure that all pupils were taught in appropriate academic sets between which movements could be made as necessary. In school X, there was no need for changes in teaching groups during the first year, as a withdrawal system catered for the individual problems of slow learning pupils.

3.7 The Extent of Slow Learner Provision in Selected Schools

In view of the fact that the procedures employed and the tests used to identify slow learners varied considerably throughout the sample, it was considered necessary to find a means by which slow learners in different schools might be compared. As pupils entered secondary schools at 11+, 12+, 13+ and 14+, a test was sought which was suitable for pupils in the 11 to 14 chronological age range and which discriminated at the lower ability levels. The numbers of tests which contained these elements and were also straightforward to administer were few. The final choice was *Young's Spar Reading Test*. This is a timed, 13 minute test consisting of 15 pictorial and 30 written items which increase in difficulty throughout the test. It is designed for pupils aged between seven and 15 years 11 months and discriminates at the lower ability levels. However its usefulness as a means of identifying slow learners is limited by the item content, as scores give only an indication of pupils' ability to decode and, by recognition, to select the correct word to complete a sentence. The pupil is not required to construct a response, to write or to spell. Thus the test was not used to 'define' slow learners or to identify all pupils with learning difficulties, as results could not show many of the problem areas which were the concern of remedial staff. Consequently, it is probable that the *Spar* test results underestimated the numbers of pupils who were experiencing difficulties in the classroom. Another limitation of the test is that it does not discriminate above a reading age of 10.8 years. Any pupil scoring more than 42 out of a possible 45 is merely recorded as having a reading age of more than 10.8 years. Tables are provided in the manual for converting raw score and chronological age to a reading quotient for pupils aged 7.0 to 15.11 years, but these tables extend only to the raw score of 43 out of 45 which was achieved by a large percentage of the pupils tested.

In this study, the test results of 2302 pupils aged 11+ were analysed. These were first year pupils in eleven secondary schools and third year pupils in two middle schools, situated in different parts of England and Wales. As all of the 2302 pupils were aged between 11 years 5 months and 12 years 7 months at the time of testing it was felt that reading ages were more illuminative than quotients. The results are shown in Table 3.7.

It was found that 34 per cent of the 2302 pupils tested had a reading age of 10.8 years or less and that there were wide variations in the percentages of pupils with reading ages below their chronological age in individual schools. This ranged from 62 per cent of pupils in school B to 22 per cent in school I. It was significant that many of the pupils tested had reading ages of 9.5 years or less, i.e. at least two years behind their chronological age, and such pupils would undoubtedly be experiencing difficuties in reading. Table 3.7 shows that 17 per cent of the 2302 pupils tested had a reading age of 9.5 years or less and that this ranged from 36 per cent of the year intake in school B to seven per cent in school L.

Five of the schools with large numbers of pupils with low reading ages and consequently with reading problems, B, H, G, A and K, were in social priority areas. School B, with a large immigrant population, and school H, in an overspill area, had the highest percentages of pupils with reading ages of 10.8 or less, i.e. one year

Table 3.7: *Percentage of pupils aged 11+ with reading ages of 10.8 years or less*

School	No. of Pupils Tested	Pupils Scoring						Total Pupils Scoring	
		9.5 or less		9.6–10.0		10.1–10.8		10.8 or less	
		N	%	N	%	N	%	N	%
Secondary									
A	99	22	(22)	6	(6)	9	(9)	37	(37)
B	163	58	(36)	17	(10)	26	(16)	1101	(62)
C	208	24	(11)	13	(6)	16	(8)	53	(25)
D	200	28	(14)	13	(6)	19	(10)	60	(30)
E	120	16	(13)	3	(3)	12	(10)	31	(26)
F	239	33	(14)	14	(6)	33	(14)	80	(34)
G	193	40	(21)	17	(8)	30	(16)	87	(45)
H	179	63	(35)	14	(8)	20	(11)	97	(54)
I	192	19	(10)	11	(5)	13	(7)	43	(22)
J	293	31	(11)	16	(5)	24	(8)	71	(24)
K	197	34	(17)	17	(9)	15	(8)	66	(34)
Middle									
L	79	6	(7)	6	(7)	10	(13)	22	(27)
M	140	24	(17)	8	(6)	17	(12)	49	(35)
	2302	398	(17)	155	(7)	244	(10)	792	(34)

or more below chronological age: 62 per cent and 54 per cent respectively. These two schools also had the greatest proportion of pupils with reading ages of 9.5 or less: 36 and 35 per cent respectively. School G was also located in an overspill area, and almost half of the pupils in the first year had reading ages of 10.8 years or less and 21 per cent had reading ages of 9.5 or less. In schools A and K, which were both urban schools sited in depressed areas, the problems appeared to be less severe, as approximately one-third of the intake in each school had a reading age of 10.8 or less. However, it should not be inferred that only schools sited in city, urban or overspill areas receive many pupils with low reading ages; school M, for example, which was located in a rural area, had a similar percentage of pupils with reading problems to school K.

The scores from the *Spar Reading Test* are given in Table 3.8 and

Table 3.8: *Reading ages (Spar) of pupils tested (T) and numbers of pupils for whom remedial provision was made (P).*

School	7 or less T	P	7.1–7.5 T	P	7.6–8.0 T	P	8.1–8.5 T	P	8.6–9.0 T	P	9.1–9.5 T	P	9.6–10.0 T	P	10.1–10.8 T	P	>10.8 T	P	Total T	P
Secondary																				
A	1	(1)	1	(1)	4	(4)	4	(4)	1	(1)	11	(1)	6	(1)	9	–	62	–	99	(13)
B	2	(2)	3	(3)	8	(8)	15	(15)	14	(14)	16	(13)	17	(11)	26	(6)	62	(6)	163	(78)
C	–	–	2	(2)	4	(3)	2	(2)	7	(7)	9	(6)	13	(7)	16	(2)	155	(5)	208	(35)
D	1	(1)	3	(3)	8	(8)	7	(3)	4	(3)	5	(3)	13	(6)	19	(4)	140	(7)	200	(38)
E	2	(2)	–	–	1	(1)	3	(2)	5	(5)	5	(3)	3	–	12	(2)	89	–	120	(15)
F	–	–	2	(2)	6	(6)	11	(11)	7	(7)	7	(5)	14	(7)	33	(6)	159	(7)	239	(51)
G	–	–	–	–	8	(8)	9	(9)	9	(9)	14	(13)	17	(12)	30	(15)	106	(16)	193	(82)
H	1	(1)	3	(3)	19	(17)	14	(11)	9	(8)	17	(7)	14	(4)	20	(5)	82	(4)	179	(60)
I	–	–	1	(1)	2	(2)	3	(3)	4	(4)	9	(6)	11	(7)	13	(4)	149	(8)	192	(35)
J	1	(1)	3	(3)	4	(4)	6	(6)	9	(7)	8	(7)	16	(12)	24	(11)	222	(29)	293	(80)
K	4	(4)	4	(4)	7	(6)	7	(5)	6	(2)	6	(3)	17	–	15	(2)	13	–	197	(26)
Middle																				
L	–	–	–	–	1	(1)	–	–	2	(2)	3	(2)	6	–	10	–	57	–	79	(3)
M	1	(1)	1	(1)	3	(3)	6	(4)	5	(4)	8	(4)	8	(1)	17	(1)	91	–	140	(19)
	13	(13)	23	(23)	75	(71)	87	(75)	82	(71)	118	(73)	155	(68)	244	(58)	1505	(82)	2302	(534)
	13	(13)	36	(36)	111	(107)	198	(182)	280	(253)	398	(326)	553	(394)	797	(452)	2302	(534)	2302	(534)

Example: Six pupils in school A had a reading age of 8.0 years or below and all were given remedial help, whereas in school C five of the six pupils with a reading age of 8.0 years or below were catered for and one was not given remedial tuition.

the numbers in brackets indicate the pupils for whom remedial provision was made in each school. It can be seen from Table 3.8 that not only did the number of pupils with reading ages of 10.8 or less vary considerably between schools but so also did the number and spread of pupils who were receiving remedial help. All pupils with reading age scores of 7.5 or less were receiving help. For pupils with reading ages between 7.6 and 10.8 the percentage receiving help gradually decreased; 95 per cent of pupils with a reading age of 7.6 to 8.0, 86 per cent of pupils with a reading age between 8.1 and 9.0, 62 per cent of those with a reading age of 9.1 to 9.5, 44 per cent of those with a reading age of 9.6 to 10.0 and only 24 per cent of those whose reading age was between 10.1 to 10.8. In some schools pupils with reading ages of more than 10.8 on the *Spar* test were receiving remedial help, and it is likely that these pupils had other problems not identified by this test.

There were many interwoven factors which influenced the extent of the remedial provision made in the schools. The main factors appeared to be the number of remedial staff available and the size of the group or class. As explained in Chapter two, slow learners in the first year were given remedial help in withdrawal groups, special classes or sets, or combinations of these. Table 3.9 shows the percentage of pupils receiving remedial tuition in case study schools and relates this to the form of provision organized.

When provision was made by withdrawing pupils for literacy skills only, it was possible for a few remedial teachers to give help to a large number of pupils. At school H, for example, where 54 per cent of pupils appeared to have reading problems, the remedial department of only one full-time and two part-time staff, withdrawing pupils from the first three years, provided help in literacy skills for 60 pupils in the first year. It was school policy for slow learners to be withdrawn in groups of three or four. As indicated by the *Spar Test*, there were probably 37 other pupils who needed help, but in order to meet their need by this system of provision either more remedial staff would be required or the size of the withdrawal groups would have to increase.

When special classes existed, particularly when the remedial department was responsible for teaching a number of subjects to slow learners in several year groups, large numbers of remedial teachers were necessary. In school G, for instance, 13 remedial staff were responsible for teaching most subjects to four special classes in

Table 3.9: *Organization of slow learner provision: pupils aged 11+ with a reading age of 10.8 years or less (Spar) and pupils for whom slow learner provision was made*

School	Provision for Slow Learners	Number of Pupils Aged 11+	Number and Percentage of Pupils Aged 11+ Scoring 10.8 or Less		Number and Percentage of Pupils Aged 11+ For Whom Provision Was Made	
			N	%	N	%
G	4 special classes	193	87	(45)	82	(42)
J	4 special classes	293	71	(24)	80	(27)
B	5 special classes	163	101	(62)	78	(48)
I	1 special class + withdrawal	192	43	(22)	35	(18)
H	Withdrawal	179	97	(54)	60	(33)
F	Withdrawal	239	80	(33)	51	(21)
C	Withdrawal	208	53	(25)	34	(16)
D	Sets	200	60	(30)	38	(19)
E	Sets	120	31	(26)	15	(13)
K	3 special classes + withdrawal	197	66	(34)	26	(13)
M	1 special class	140	49	(35)	19	(14)
A	1 special class	99	37	(37)	13	(13)
L	Withdrawal	79	22	(28)	3	(4)

each of the first three years, two special classes in year 4 and two in year 5. Forty-five per cent of pupils in the first year had a reading age of 10.8 or less according to the *Spar* test, and the school made provision for 82 out of these 87 pupils by allocating an average of 20 pupils to each of the four special classes.

Where the school policy was to organize special classes and few remedial staff were available, there was a danger that some of the pupils who needed help would not receive it. In school A, for example, where three remedial staff were responsible for teaching a number of subjects in one special class in each of years 1 to 5, only 13 pupils were placed in the special class and yet it appeared from the results of the *Spar* test that up to 37 pupils in the year needed remedial help. Thus three remedial teachers, together with the school's policy of keeping the special class small, meant that although pupils with the most severe problems were given help in this class, other pupils, some of whom had reading ages of less than 9.5 years, were not receiving any remedial tuition.

School K was another example of a school where the policy of small special classes for slow learners limited the extent of the provision made. Although 66 pupils appeared to have some reading problems, only 26 pupils had been allocated to the special classes. One of the eight remedial teachers was employed to withdraw pupils from classes for extra reading but this did little to increase the extent of remedial provision because withdrawal took place mainly from within the remedial band.

The use of a combination of special classes and withdrawal for slow learners was adopted by many schools. In school I, for example, one part-time and three full-time teachers were responsible for special classes in years 1 to 3 and also for the withdrawal of pupils from the mainstream. In the first year, 15 pupils with severe difficulties were placed in the special class and a further 20 were withdrawn in groups of two or three from mainstream classes for help with literacy skills. In this way two types of provision met pupils' different needs and 35 out of the 43 pupils who appeared to have reading problems were able to receive remedial help.

Different combinations of the three elements − type of provision, size of pupil group and staff deployment − were found to influence the number of slow learners for whom provision was made. In some small schools, staffing was the dominant factor; for example school M had only one remedial teacher who was responsible for the English/literacy skills of slow learners aged 11+ and 12+ who had been allocated to special classes. The *Spar* test showed that in this school approximately 35 per cent of pupils aged 11+ had some reading problems but that only 14 per cent of this year group were in the special class. These 19 pupils had reading ages ranging from less thn 7.0 up to 10.8 years and yet there were seven other pupils in the year with reading ages of between 8.1 and 9.5 years. An unfavourable staff ratio of 1:22 in this small school limited the adjustments which could be made to group size or to organization in order to extend the remedial help available or to provide individual or small group tuition. Requests to the LEA for help had resulted in the arrival of a peripatetic teacher who coached pupils with the lowest reading ages. However, there remained a number of pupils who appeared to need help but who were receiving none.

3.8 Discussion

Some schools enrolled many pupils whose reading ages were behind their chronological ages by one, two or more than two years. The extent of the reading problems experienced by slow learners in case study schools was explored using the results of the *Spar Reading Test*. As previously indicated, this simple test was not used in an attempt to 'define' the slow learner; the results gave information about reading ability only and for this reason probably underestimated the extent of learning difficulties among pupils in these schools. However it provided a means by which widely varying percentages of pupils aged 11+ with low reading ages in case study schools could be identified. Further investigation revealed that in some schools pupils with reading ages of over 10.8 years were receiving help, while in others there were pupils with reading ages of less than 9.5 for whom no remedial provision was made.

This highlights the problem facing secondary schools with each new intake. For although the research identified evidence of considerable liaison between secondary schools and their feeders, the value to secondary staff of much of the test information received can be questioned. Test data were found to be so varied as to be unreliable indicators for both class placement and as a means of identifying pupils with learning problems. Thus while secondary staff were made aware of those pupils from each feeder whose standard of attainment was below the average for their peer group, in many cases it was found necessary to re-test shortly after entry to secondary school as the information on file was not strictly comparable. Marks from school-based tests and exams were similarly problematic. Teachers' comments were considered useful and many staff found visits to feeder schools particularly helpful in alerting them to the needs of individual pupils.

Each year the numbers of new entrants with learning difficulties admitted to a given secondary school will vary. The miscellany of test information received from feeder schools does not provide a particularly helpful source for those who allocate pupils to teaching groups. Staff were found to be hampered in their attempts to place pupils and to diagnose their needs by a shortage of up-to-date published tests and a paucity of information concerning the contents of those which were on the market. Two strands emerge. First, there is an urgent requirement for the production of up-to-date tests which will diagnose the problems of pupils with learning difficulties and for tests which will discriminate at the lower end of the ability range for pupils aged 11+. Such tests could be incorporated into a profiling system which would provide secondary school staff with a fuller and more reliable source of information than that at present commonly available at transfer. The second strand concerns transfer between primary and secondary sectors. With advantage, systematic procedures for use at the time of transition could be devised, either at local authority level or by secondary schools in co-operation with their feeders, a practice already being developed in some LEAs. This would provide secondary schools with a comprehensive source of information based on specified tests which would be of immense value to staff concerned with pupil placement and with the identification of those with learning difficulties upon entry.

The final section of the chapter, in which the numbers of slow learners for whom provision was made were compared with the numbers present who had low reading ages, revealed the influences of grouping policy and staffing levels and deployment on the numbers of pupils for whom it was possible to cater. Certain grouping systems, in particular the special class, obviously afforded less flexibility than some withdrawal systems as they 'tied up' remedial staff with relatively few pupils. However, the question of whether to teach a small special group or to help pupils individually is a question which each school must resolve for itself. Decisions on the balancing of resources in terms of curriculum, time and staff can only be made by those most closely involved with slow learner provision.

Chapter four

Teachers in Charge of Slow Learner Provision

4.1 Administrative Structure

The different kinds of slow learner provision described in Chapter two were, in 76 per cent of schools, mediated through remedial departments. In 15 per cent of schools provision was organized by a group of teachers who did not in themselves constitute a separate department; in eight per cent one member of staff was appointed with special responsibility for slow learning pupils and in the remaining one per cent of schools slow learning pupils were catered for within one or more of the subject departments or by means of a remedial teacher from the local authority peripatetic team.

In this chapter the role of the head of department or teacher in charge of slow learner provision is explored, details of the curricular areas for which such departments are commonly found to be responsible are given and their role, as outlined in school documents to parents, is examined. In the responses received from schools concerning 'the education of slow learning pupils between the ages of 11 and 18', as defined in our questionnaire, it was apparent that the terms 'slow learner' and 'remedial' were, in many cases, used synonymously. Responsibility for all or part of the education of slow learning pupils most commonly lay with the teacher or group of staff who provided the school's 'remedial' teaching support. In some cases, the work of these 'remedial' departments also included the provision of work for more able pupils who were failing in a particular area of the curriculum, while in others compensatory education was provided for pupils who were learning English and in a few cases, individual learning opportunities were available for 'high fliers' requiring extension work. Thus the group of slow learners who constitute the focus of this enquiry were not necessarily the only members of a special department within the school, but were most usually catered for by a 'remedial' department or by teachers experienced in remedial work. Throughout this chapter, the schools' terminology is used for quotation purposes and the terms 'teachers of slow learners' and 'remedial teachers' are used synonymously.

The data are drawn from two sources: questionnaires and case studies. The former provided most of the information from a sample of 791 schools and 1467 teachers of slow learners and the latter were used to explore more fully the workings of a department and in particular the role of its head. Table 4.1 shows that slow learner departments ranged from small units run by one person to teams of up to 13 teachers. In many schools, subject specialists who taught slow learners for part of their timetable were also affiliated to the department, joining in regular departmental meetings and attending case conferences on individual pupils as required. The teacher in charge of slow learner provision was therefore responsible not only for those appointed primarily to teach slow learners but also for the work of those subject staff who taught groups of slow learning pupils.

With wide variation in the sizes of schools and in the kind of provision offered to slow learners, it is not surprising that the numbers of teachers in slow learner departments as shown in Table 4.1 displayed a considerable range. Most of the small schools with fewer than 500 pupils employed one or two members of staff to cater for slow learners while the majority of schools with over 1200 pupils on roll provided departments of three, four or more teachers for this purpose. However, while one comprehensive with over 1750 pupils employed two staff to teach slow learners, a much smaller one with fewer than 750 pupils had a large department of ten. It must be remembered that differences in catchment areas can result in some schools receiving more pupils who have learning difficulties than others; also, as Chapter three indicates, the way in which staff are deployed to help pupils with learning difficulties throughout the school has a considerable impact on the slow learner staffing establishment. For example, two comprehensive schools in the survey, each with over 1000 pupils on roll, made very different provision for slow learners. One concentrated efforts in the first year, withdrawing pupils for individual tuition and returning them

Table 4.1: *Schools with slow learner departments: size of school and size of department*

No. of Staff in Department	Number of Pupils on the School Roll								Total
	<251	251–500	501–750	751–1000	1001–1250	1251–1500	1501–1750	>1750|	
1	1	28	34	24	19	5	0	0	111
2	1	18	49	56	48	10	2	1	185
3	0	5	24	43	34	13	6	2	127
4	0	3	15	21	18	20	5	1	83
5	0	2	2	9	7	8	9	1	38
6–9	0	0	5	7	14	11	7	2	46
10–13	0	0	1	0	2	3	3	1	10
Total	2	56	130	160	142	70	32	8	600

† One school had more than 2000 pupils on roll.
No response – 3 schools.

to the mainstream as appropriate. Fifteen per cent of pupils in the entry year were helped in this way by one part-time and two full-time remedial teachers but very few pupils were withdrawn regularly from subsequent years, although the facility was available from years 1 to 5 and pupils could be referred for diagnostic testing at any time. In contrast, slow learner classes were established in the other comprehensive, catering for 13 per cent of new entrants and for between 11 and 14 per cent of each year group up to and including the 5th year. Eight full-time remedial staff were necessary to maintain this level of provision. The school received a social priority allowance and approximately one-fifth of all new entrants arrived with reading ages two years or more behind their chronological ages. It should therefore be remembered that the tasks of a teacher in charge of special provision are likely to vary in scale, if not in nature, depending on the range and severity of the problems experienced among slow learning pupils.

4.2 Slow Learner Departments

As expected, approximately three-quarters of the departments (74 per cent) were simply called 'Remedial', but a number of other names were also adopted. 'Compensatory Studies', 'Special Education', 'Basic Studies', 'General Studies', 'Combined Studies' and 'Integrated Studies' accounted for a further 13 per cent of the sample. Other departments were entitled 'Progress', 'Opportunity', 'Learning Difficulties Department', 'Coaching Department', the 'Department of Special Educational Resources' and the 'Individual Learning Unit'. Other names included the 'Literacy and Numeracy Department', the 'Department of Special Needs', 'The Help Centre' and the 'Tutorial Centre'. In one school the department was named after a past member of staff and in another after the teaching block in which the suite of rooms was located.

School handbooks provided insights into the kind of role that these departments were designed to fulfil. In some publications special help was briefly mentioned: for example, 'We provide coaching in basic skills for all who need it', while in a few schools a paragraph or more outlined the work of the department.

The following extracts are all drawn from school handbooks for parents. The first describes a remedial department within the faculty of language, of which the head of faculty wrote:

> We work very closely with the remedial department and from the start students who require special help with reading are withdrawn for extra attention.

The head of the remedial department explained that pupils were withdrawn from English lessons and taught in small groups, rejoining their class as soon as possible. A slightly different role was fulfilled by another remedial department whose head wrote:

> Most help is given during the first two years, with teaching normally taking place in small groups extracted from English and mathematics. In other subjects such as science, the teacher goes into the department and provides support in the classroom situation.

In another school, provision for slow learners was made within a department called the individual learning unit, whose two staff also assisted colleagues in designing resource materials for less able pupils in mixed ability classes. A similar but slightly wider brief was held by another department whose head explained that she co-ordinated the activities of a team of teachers drawn from all areas of the school which provided a variety of materials suitable for individual learning programmes.

In several of the documents we received, emphasis was placed on remedial teachers working outside their department and helping mainstream staff, together with an acknowledgement that remedial teachers were concerned with areas of pupils' personal development as well as with their achievement in the basic skills. A document from one school exemplified this:

> The personal touch is really what the unit is all about. Strong personal links between teachers and children, teachers and parents and between teachers and support agencies provide an effective working relationship.

Information received from 397 secondary and 50 middle schools revealed that while English/literacy skills were taught by every department and by every group of teachers with special responsibility for slow learner provision, maths/numeracy skills were offered by remedial staff in approximately half of the schools surveyed, humanities and social studies by one quarter while very few remedial departments were responsible for teaching other subjects such as craft, European studies, PE or science to slow learning pupils. The teacher in charge of slow learner provision was therefore primarily concerned with the language, number and humanities areas of the curriculum. Detailed accounts of the curricula offered to slow learners in specific schools are given in Chapters six and seven.

4.3 The Role of the Head of the Slow Learner Department

The 17 schools visited by the team varied in both their mainstream organization and in the way in which provision was made for slow learners; differences which were reflected in the roles of those appointed with special responsibility for slow pupils. The influence of age range and type of catchment is also relevant in this context; for example, some departments were large and catered for half of the first year intake where it was felt that the degree of learning difficulty among new entrants called for remedial help on a major scale. Two of the case study schools coped with large numbers of slow learners by organizing several special classes in the intake year with correspondingly large numbers of staff allocated to the remedial department. In other schools, staff identified very few entrants with learning difficulties which would classify them as slow learners, one head estimating that the proportion of slow learners was as low as 5 per cent of the school roll. In cases such as this, fewer staff were allocated to remedial education and a smaller proportion of the school's resources were devoted to the needs of slow learners, with obvious implications for the role of the head of such a department.

In 1979 the National Association for Remedial Education (NARE) published a handbook entitled 'The Role of Remedial Teachers' in which the role of the head of a remedial department was clearly spelled out.

> In addition to supervising colleagues these teachers would advise head teachers about such matters as curriculum content, resources and materials and school organization in relation to work with children with learning difficulties. They would also be responsible for the organization and supervision of surveys carried out by their own junior colleagues or other members of school staff, besides carrying out individual testing themselves. They would need to be capable of leading case conferences about individual children and to be responsible for the selection of children for remedial education. It is envisaged that teachers with this degree of responsibility would contribute to the in-service training of less experienced colleagues. (NARE, *Guidelines 2*, 1979)

In addition, it was stated that the specialist remedial teacher should fulfil several functions. A five point model was presented in which the assessment, prescriptive, teaching, supportive and liaison roles of the remedial teacher were outlined and the authors went on to say, 'we are aware that many colleagues are already operating effectively in more than one of these areas. It is still all too rare, however, to find many examples where they have been allowed to operate effectively in all five.' (NARE, 1979).

It is proposed in this section of the chapter to explore the role of the head of department as exemplified by the teachers in charge of slow learner provision in case study schools, using as a model the five areas NARE defined as being part of the role of every remedial teacher. This is followed by an examination of those duties identified by NARE as specific to heads of department.

Of the seventeen schools visited by the team, two were middle schools (9–13) and the remainder secondary, twelve catering for entry at 11+, one at 12+ and two at 13+. Neither of the middle schools had a head of remedial department; instead, responsibility in one school was shared between three members of the English staff and in the other a part-time teacher was appointed specifically for remedial withdrawal work. All held scale 1 posts. Thirteen of the secondary schools had a head of department appointed on scale 2, 3, 4 or the Senior Teacher Scale, leading teams which varied in size from three to 13 people. In the remaining two schools, learning advisers, one on scale 3, the other on scale 4, had been appointed with responsibility for the learning needs of all pupils. Throughout this section of the chapter, for simplicity, the 15 members of staff in secondary schools are referred to as 'heads of department', while the middle school staff are identified as 'teachers with special responsibility for slow learners'.

4.4 Assessment and Diagnosis

We turn now to the first of the five aspects which NARE suggests should be part of the role of every remedial teacher, the assessment role. This is stated to include:

(i)   The supervision and correct administration of the standardized tests as part of a comprehensive screening procedure.
(ii)   The follow up and diagnosis of specific learning difficulties in children who are identified as being 'at risk'.

(NARE, 1979)

Every one of the 15 heads of department was responsible for identifying slow learners in the new intake and for undertaking personally or supervising the diagnosis of specific learning difficulties. Twelve of the heads of department also visited feeder schools during the summer term preceding pupils entry in order to perform a variety of tasks; for example, to administer tests, to discuss individual cases with the staff, to talk to the children or to see them at work. Three heads of department used these visits as an opportunity to gather information for their own departmental records, adding to details already forwarded to the school. One teacher who had found from past experience that primary staff tended to be 'too kind' in their gradings, discussed individual pupils with the head in an attempt to learn more about those pupils whom she considered likely to need help but who had not been so identified by the school. Another head of department in a school with a large intake of Asian immigrants made visits to each feeder school in order to identify those pupils who would require special help with language. Frequently, such pupils failed to register on standardized language tests and in order to identify them, the school had devised its own methods. The head of department asked all pupils to write answers to simple oral questions and then to take down a short passage of dictation. Together with her observations of how pupils approached these tasks, the head of department identified pupils who had difficulty in writing and problems with listening skills and in spelling. Within the department, provision was subsequently made for slow learners and for those for whom English was a second language.

Seven heads of department organized the screening of the whole of the new intake with standardized tests and one set a school-originated task for all pupils as a 'fail safe mechanism' to see if any were wrongly placed. Pupils were required to produce a piece of free writing, the subject of which was immaterial (last time it was 'the family'), for assessment by the head of department. One head of department tested only those who were allocated to the slow learner class by the head of year and another tested only those pupils who had not been screened during the preceding summer term in order to complete the school's records. Three heads of department, all of whom were closely involved with the initial identification of slow learners on entry as well as their placement in special classes and sets, were not involved with screening in the secondary school but had supervised testing in feeder schools in the preceding summer term. In two schools diagnostic testing took place in English and maths some weeks after entry but was not the responsibility of the head of remedial education.

To summarize, it would appear that in the majority of secondary schools visited the assessment and diagnosis of learning difficulties among new entrants was a firmly established part of the head of department's role. A similar picture emerged from the wider sample, in which 82 per cent of heads of department reported that they used tests to identify slow learners in the new intake (Chapter three).

4.5 A Prescriptive Role

Turning to the second aspect of a remedial teacher's role, we find that NARE sees the work of the head of department as extending to advising the head on curriculum, resources and materials suitable for slow learners and discussing the organization of groups in relation to provision for slow learners. In other words, the NARE Committee consider that the head of department should be involved in policy making at the highest level, taking part in the formulation as well as the administration of school policy.

For all teachers, the prescriptive role is said to include:

(i)   The preparation and implementation of individualized pro-
       grammes for children with particular learning difficulties.
(ii)   The preparation and implementation of school strategies
       in the basic subject areas.
(iii) Costing such exercises and requisitioning accordingly.

(NARE, 1979)

In the case study schools, two strands emerged concerning the preparation and implementation of individualized programmes for pupils with particular learning difficulties. Seven schools in which there were special classes for slow learners had a head of department who drew up the syllabus to be followed by all remedial staff; in some cases this covered literacy and numeracy, in others it extended to include humanities and European studies. Seven heads of department, all of whom operated a withdrawal system, designed special literacy programmes for individual pupils, and in two schools visited, the head of department undertook both tasks. In only one school was the designing of individual programmes delegated by the learning adviser to the member of the remedial staff who saw and taught the pupils.

With regard to the formulation and implementation of school policy concerning slow learners it should be noted that approximately one in every two of the heads of department visited was on a scale 4 appointment or above, compared with one in seven of the other heads of slow learner departments in the sample. It was therefore to be expected that most of the staff visited took part in management decisions at a senior level. Heads of slow learner departments were members of teams concerned with curriculum development, testing, the guidance system and with the structuring and presentation of in-service courses; one was on a committee which met to consider the special problems faced by non English-speaking Asian pupils and eleven were members of lower school management teams. All attended heads of department meetings and all called meetings of their own specialist team to discuss both school and departmental matters. These meetings varied from informal gatherings during break or lunch-times to more formal meetings, some of which were minuted, held once or twice a term.

All of those teachers in charge of slow learner provision ordered resources for use with slow learners and in larger departments the head of department also vetted and processed requests from colleagues. In most schools, capitation was allocated to departments via the teacher in charge of slow learner provision but in three schools visited some subject departments and the library also received capitation finance specifically for slow learners. It was most usual for an annual sum to be allocated to the remedial department although in three cases there was no set sum; instead, materials were requested and needs met as far as was possible in the light of other departments' requirements. In six schools some additional funds were made available from a variety of sources which included the Parent Teacher Association and the LEA, and one head of department mentioned that the remedial staff sometimes engaged in their own fund raising activities in order to buy additional resources for use with slow learners.

In the whole sample, the financing of slow learner provision revealed a similar pattern, as 42 per cent of secondary school departments received an annual allowance in the form of a sum of money and a further 22 per cent of teachers in charge of slow learner provision indicated that the amount was open to negotiation from year to year. In only nine per cent of schools was it usual for specific materials to be requested and four per cent of schools financed slow learner provision by other means, primarily via subject departments. In 23 per cent of schools the system involved a combination of both an allocation of money and requests for items of equipment.

4.6 A Teaching/Therapeutic Role

Three aspects of this part of the remedial teacher's role were identified by NARE. These were:

(i)   Teaching individuals and groups where the nature of the problem makes it impossible for it to be contained within the normal classroom situation.

(ii) Treating children with associated behavioural difficulties.

(iii) Where appropriate, co-operating with other colleagues on a team teaching basis.

(NARE, 1979)

All of the heads of department in the secondary schools visited taught slow learners in classes, groups or individually, dealing primarily with problems of reading, spelling, writing and computational skills. The teachers spent between 20 per cent and 100 per cent of their teaching time with slow learners. Nine heads of department taught slow learners exclusively, five spent a few lessons in the mainstream each week, and one, who was the learning adviser for the whole ability range, taught more mainstream classes than slow learner groups. Subjects taught to slow learners by heads of department in case study schools included literacy, numeracy and general subjects; one member of staff gave lessons in conversational French and two ran a record of personal achievement scheme for pupils in the 4th and 5th year.

The treatment of children with behavioural as well as learning difficulties was a recognized part of the teaching role of the heads of department as well as of all other remedial staff, although teachers emphasized in interview that remedial departments were not designed for pupils with behavioural or maladjustment problems alone. These pupils were referred to the pastoral system or to a special unit, but slow learners who also exhibited behavioural problems were catered for by remedial department staff in every school visited. The association between learning difficulties and behavioural problem is well known, and it was observed that some of the pupils in the departments required a great deal of individual attention and direction, and that the behaviours exhibited in order to gain this attention would undoubtedly have caused problems and possibly disruption in an ordinary classroom or in a larger group. There was a degree of informality, made possible by the smaller size of the groups, and it was noted that slow learners were encouraged to take responsibility for their own learning programmes by self-marking and keeping records of completed tasks, collecting the resources required for each section of work and returning them to the appropriate place after use.

There was one department which provided extra help for pupils with behavioural problems whereby individual pupils were withdrawn from mainstream classes for one week and given a work programme closely supervised by one member of the remedial team. This system enabled any learning difficulties to be identified but was primarily designed to offer the opportunity for counselling. After one week the pupil returned to mainstream lessons, liaison having taken place between all staff concerned, i.e. remedial teachers, form tutor and subject specialists.

The third aspect of the remedial teacher's role, that of co-operation with colleagues on a team teaching basis, was found to take place in two ways. First, teaching as a team with other members of the department proved to be a feature of a few of the withdrawal systems and two heads of department saw this as a valuable in-service training exercise; second, working beside subject teachers outside the department and providing support for any pupils who were having problems in the ordinary classroom was a feature built into the organization of special provision in two of the 15 schools visited. Support was given in lower school English, maths and humanities lessons. While much has been written in recent years about the growth of this aspect of the work of the remedial teacher, the project identified only 21 schools out of 791 in which this kind of co-operation and support was present: less than 3 per cent of the sample. In a few cases, heads stated that recent cutbacks in the staffing establishment had forced them to cease this method of support for slow learners.

4.7 A Supportive Role

This was defined by NARE as advising colleagues on:

(i) Appropriate grouping/setting procedures.
(ii) Ideas and techniques for the range of children with special educational needs.

(iii) The range of materials and apparatus available.
(iv) Remedial work 'across the curriculum'.

(NARE, 1979)

Nine heads of department were involved in the allocation of slow learners to special classes, sets and mixed ability teaching groups, joining the management team who worked together made up the teaching and tutor groups for each new intake. Two of those not involved with initial placements employed standardized tests to establish the nature of learning difficulties among pupils allocated to the remedial department and to decide on the most appropriate grouping procedures. The third tested the whole intake in order to identify slow learners for withdrawal into small groups for special teaching. Remedial staff were not observed to advise subject specialists on grouping procedures for use within subject departments. In one school, however, 4th year option lists compiled by subject staff were passed to the remedial adviser before they were finalized. The adviser was asked to comment on the suitability of subject choices and the subsequent allocation to option classes of those pupils who had been withdrawn to receive educational support in the lower school. This was found to be a most helpful way of ensuring that slow learning pupils were following a balanced curriculum at an appropriate level in their final years at school.

In the whole sample of 791 schools, it was rare to find a remedial teacher or head of department whose role included the giving of support to other staff who required specific remedial help with more able pupils and there were few heads of department who were responsible for the special needs of pupils from across the whole ability range. However, three such staff were included in case studies in order that this aspect of their role might be more fully explored. It was found that while all children with special educational needs were the responsibility of two learning advisers and one head of department, ideas and techniques for such pupils were not widely disseminated by any of them. In one of these three schools, specific responsibility for more able pupils was delegated to another senior member of staff and in the other two the head of department was consulted for advice on particular pupils as the need arose. In all of the other schools visited the head of department had responsibility for slow learning pupils and for those with learning difficulties arising from English being a second language but not for more able pupils with specific problems. This led us to the conclusion that the wider role of 'learning adviser for all pupils with special educational needs' is poorly developed in secondary schools and moreover it is a role which few heads of remedial departments can readily fulfil.

The third aspect of the supportive role concerned the giving of advice to colleagues on the range of materials and apparatus available. This was found to operate on two levels. Within remedial departments there was usually a ready exchange of ideas and information on resource materials but the team found only one example out of the 15 where remedial staff drew the attention of subject teachers to published resource materials suitable for less able pupils. Even here the value of this advice was questioned. As the teacher in charge of slow learner provision explained:

> You can recommend suitable resources but there is no guarantee that anyone will use them.

The influence of remedial staff on achieving remedial work 'across the curriculum' varied considerably between schools. In one school where slow learners were taught in special classes for English and maths, a working party resulting from a head of department meeting about the needs of slow learners had recommended the examination of each subject area and had rewritten the syllabus for first year pupils. Aims and objectives for each course were listed, the concepts taught were set out, the skills used were itemized and essential vocabulary specified. 'The aim of the operation was to try to identify the weaknesses of many of our pupils as a first step to fostering a co-operative interdepartmental attempt to remedy them.' A document circulated to all staff contained the following introduction:

> These summary syllabuses for year 1 are offered to the whole staff in the hope of promoting a sense of the necessarily co-operative nature of the school as a learning experience. Do take up in your lessons any links possible with other subject areas.

Thus co-operation was encouraged between subject staff as well as between the remedial department and other subject areas.

From case study observations it would appear that the supportive aspect of the remedial teacher's role differed considerably from school to school, dependent not only on the official role as expressed in the title of the head of department but also influenced by the desire of the appointed member of staff to work outside the department. Much was seen to depend upon the degree to which the head of department, having taken the initiative in the first place, was able to sustain liaison with subject teachers on a range of topics relating to slow learners. From observation it would appear that heads of department operating withdrawal systems made this opportunity more frequently than did those teaching special classes or sets; this was not surprising in view of the fact that some liaison concerning pupil transfer took place with subject staff in most withdrawal systems anyway, but was not traditionally part of the role of those who taught special classes. Thus where there was withdrawal, staff might expect a remedial teacher to consult them about a particular pupil but these expectations would not be the same in a school where slow learners were taught in separate groups for much of the curriculum. The expectations of subject teachers together with the personality of the staff member who is responsible for slow learner provision, combined with the name and status of the remedial team or department, interact to create an environment within which the supportive role is either fostered or discouraged. The following examples illustrate the ways in which two heads of department provided support for colleagues.

School C

The head of the Individual Learning Unit (ILU) was responsible for all pupils with learning difficulties or with special needs throughout the school, whatever their ability. With this brief she attended all heads of faculty meetings and set about enlisting the aid of one representative from each faculty, to be known as a co-ordinator. The co-ordinators designed teaching materials for slow learners for use within their own faculty areas and maintained a dialogue with the individual learning department. The head of the ILU organized an in-service course for the co-ordinators at the local teachers' centre where together they discussed and designed a unit of work for slow learning pupils. With this as a starting point she found it easier to liaise with subject staff via the co-ordinator and had subsequently developed a series of learning routes at different levels through humanities topics for use in mixed ability classrooms. In this way the aim of the individual learning unit was being promoted, as its head wanted as few pupils as possible to attend on a regular basis, encouraging remedial work to take place across the curriculum and in the ordinary classroom instead. She was slowly establishing a climate within which she could work towards her aim of having very few pupils extracted from the mainstream.

School N

Here the head of department, who was called a learning adviser, had oversight of all pupils with exceptional needs: the physically-handicapped, ESN, very able pupils, slow learners and those for whom English was a second language. She had contributed to an in-service course in which the needs of slow learners were highlighted and in response to this, work had been initiated on resources in the humanities department. Teachers were encouraged to discuss existing teaching materials with the adviser, with a view to redesigning them for use with the full ability range. In rewriting these teaching materials special care was taken over the language used and the layout adopted.

Staff were encouraged to use a range of resources and a variety of teaching methods in order to meet the needs of slow learners in a mixed ability class and a booklet on teaching slow learners produced by the learning adviser contained practical advice on classroom management and resource production. When 4th year option groups were being made up the learning adviser commented on those pupils who had received remedial help; information which was used by heads of department and the deputy head to guide them in the composition of option groups for CSE and GCE.

In another school a learning adviser had been appointed who ran courses for teachers new to the school, both probationers and more experienced staff, in which attention was drawn to the needs of all pupils throughout the ability range and the importance of providing appropriate resources to meet their needs. A slightly different kind of support was offered in one of the larger comprehensive schools, where pupils with problems in any subject and any year group could be sent with a work guide stating the nature of the difficulty to the head of the remedial department for short-term intensive individual help. This system extended the area of responsibility of the head of department from slow learners alone to all those pupils with learning difficulties and in so doing provided two valuable spin-offs. First, it removed the idea that the department was only designed to help 'slow' pupils and second, it provided the opportunity for liaison between subject staff and the head of department.

While all heads of department gave advice about remedial work informally to other staff and more formally at heads of department meetings, the examples described above reflect a more positive move towards the establishment of regular liaison and dialogue between subject teachers and the remedial staff, apparent in as yet only a few schools.

4.8 A Liaison Role

As outlined by NARE this included, where appropriate, liaising with:

(i)   Support services, in particular the school psychological, school health, educational welfare and careers guidance services.
(ii)   Parents.
(iii) The community at large.

(NARE, 1979)

In 12 of the 15 schools, teachers in charge of slow learner provision contacted support services directly and in the other three requests were routed through the senior management team. The adviser for special or remedial education was most frequently contacted, followed by the educational psychologist, educational welfare officer, school medical service, social services and the local teachers' centre.

Links with parents were made at parents' evenings, report evenings and open days, and several heads of department encouraged parents to visit the school to discuss any problems with them. In a number of departments, volunteer 'reading mums' visited the school regularly to hear slow learners read on a one-to-one basis. Local circumstances affected the degree of liaison with parents; for example, the head of department in one industrial town visited the homes of many of her pupils in order to deliver their reports and also to meet the parents who had been prevented by shift work from attending a report evening. Another head of department in a rural area had got to know local families over a number of years and was able to make ready contact with parents by telephone whenever she wished.

Links with the community at large again varied with local conditions. One head of department liaised with local firms in order to place pupils – some of whom were slow learners – on work experience schemes, and others made similar contacts with local establishments such as hospitals and old peoples' homes in order to give slow learners some work experience for their record of personal achievement course. One head of department kept in close touch with the local college of education, another organized a link scheme with the city's polytechnic for 4th and 5th year pupils, some of whom were slow learners, while a third liaised with a nearby language centre in order to monitor the progress of pupils who spent one hour per week there.

4.9 Slow Learner Provision in the Middle Schools

Before moving on to examine the nature of other tasks also carried out by heads of remedial departments it is pertinent to comment on the role of these staff who taught slow learners in middle schools. As mentioned earlier in this chapter, only one-third of middle schools made provision for slow learners within a special department; most were taught by English department staff and/or a peripatetic remedial teacher. In neither of the two middle schools visited was there a separate department but teachers of slow learners were involved in testing programmes; in one middle school the remedial teacher took charge of screening the new intake at 9+ with a view to identifying pupils who required help with reading and, in the other, where there was no teacher with special responsibility for slow learners, the English staff all administered the same reading test to new entrants in order to identify those with low reading ages in their own mixed ability classes. In both schools, remedial staff made use of reading tests to establish base lines and to monitor progress.

Teachers in both middle schools designed individual programmes for pupils with learning difficulties, focused on improving their literacy skills. Unlike some of their secondary school contemporaries, however, these remedial staff were not involved in policy making; they attended English department and full staff meetings but were not part of the school's management team. It should be remembered that in one school the three staff involved were all members of the English department and in the other, two were subject specialists and the teacher in charge of slow learner provision held a part-time appointment specifically for this purpose. Most work was on a withdrawal or small group basis which, from time to time, included the teaching of pupils with associated behaviour problems. In both of the middle schools, the teachers in charge were allocated a sum of money to be spent on slow learners each year and they selected and ordered new resources and equipment. All taught individuals and groups and none used any team teaching techniques.

The supportive role of the remedial teacher was observed to exist in an informal way in the middle schools, where a smaller staff made informal contacts easier to establish and maintain than in many secondary schools. Form teachers, remedial specialists and subject staff regularly discussed individual pupils at break or lunchtime and this appeared sufficient to maintain the degree of liaison deemed necessary.

Thus while aspects of the assessment, prescriptive, teaching, supportive and liaison roles were all present in middle schools, they were less developed in some respects than those in other secondary schools, a fact which was reflected in the scales of these appointments (Section 4.4).

4.10 Other Aspects of the Role of a Head of Department

The National Association of Remedial Education outlined the nature of those duties which it considered would be the responsibility of a head of department; namely, advising heads and colleagues on curriculum, resources and organization for slow learners; administering tests; supervising departmental surveys; leading case conferences and contributing to the in-service training of less experienced colleagues. All except surveys and case conferences have already been explored in the context of the role of the remedial teacher as exemplified by the heads of department in case study schools. While two of the heads of department stated that organizing case conferences was part of their work, on further enquiry it became clear that all heads of department would attend but not necessarily organize case conferences involving pupils taught by them personally or by members of their department. No evidence of surveys or small scale research was found in this sample of schools, but other activities were identified which included the organization of community service and work experience for slow learners, the giving of guidance on their option choices, in-service work with probationary teachers and the appointment of new staff to the remedial department. In addition, other items specific to particular schools included responsibility for the school's audio-visual equipment, the drawing up of individual staff and student timetables for a withdrawal system and pastoral responsibility for all 4th and 5th year pupils. One head of department was a deputy head and one of the learning advisers was also head of a subject department. In one school the head of the remedial department was the school representative on the Board of Governors.

4.11 Discussion

In exploring the role of the teacher in charge of slow learner provision, this chapter has identified certain aspects which are central to the work of all remedial staff as well as tasks which are viewed as the special responsibility of the head of department. It has highlighted some major differences in the ways in which heads of department work in schools and has shown how it is possible to involve teachers from a variety of different subject areas in the education of slow learning pupils. The chapter has also illustrated how heads of department have worked beyond school, for example, visiting feeder schools, contacting local firms and meeting parents.

The five functions outlined by NARE as part of the role of every remedial teacher were fufilled by all heads of department visited, but in varying degrees. The assessment and diagnosis of learning difficulties was unquestionably central to the work of every head of department, but the placement of slow learners in teaching and registration groups, a separate but related issue, was not. Indeed, the involvement of the head of the remedial department in allocation procedures for the new intake was less frequent than might have been expected from staff holding scale 3 or 4 head of department appointments. Nine of the seventeen heads of department in case study schools were closely involved in allocation procedures, which is a higher proportion than the 26 per cent found in the whole sample. Thus in three-quarters of the sample, teachers in charge of slow learning pupils took no part in deciding where slow learners in the new intake were to be placed for registration and/or teaching purposes. In many schools, testing took place after entry to establish the nature and extent of the learning difficulties among pupils who had already been allocated to particular teaching groups.

The prescriptive role was well developed at classroom level, where heads of department had drawn up syllabuses, some of which covered curricular areas other than basic skills, as well as individual learning programmes for pupils with literacy problems. These written syllabuses were usually prefaced by general aims and specific objectives. At management level, while several heads of department served on a variety of school committees and some were members of senior management teams, not all were involved with policy making at the level recommended by NARE. More recently, Bailey (1981) urged remedial teachers to join curriculum development teams in different subject areas in order to advise on how the curriculum might be adapted for pupils with special needs; a suggestion which some heads of department could take as a useful starting point for establishing communications with subject staff.

While it was common to find two remedial teachers working together with a group of slow learning pupils, it was not common to find remedial staff supporting subject teachers in mainstream classes in either case study schools or in the main sample of 791 schools. It was rarer still to identify schools in which the brief of the head of department extended to cover all pupils with specific learning difficulties. NARE, in the publication *Guidelines 2* (1979) states that 'remedial education is both a horizontal and vertical concept. Children carry their problems across the curriculum and long-term benefits can only be achieved within the context of genuine team effort and co-operation.' For this to work effectively it requires not only considerable work on the part of the head of department but also a willingness amongst subject teachers throughout the school to listen, to learn and to adapt. The schools in which support in the ordinary classroom was observed to be taking place all used withdrawal as part of their system of catering for slow learners and thus a tradition of informal liaison between remedial and subject teachers already existed. McCall (1977) drew attention to this aspect of the remedial teacher's work, when, in exploring a withdrawal system, he wrote 'the teacher acting as the withdrawal agent must see the supportive nature of the role and make considerable efforts to gain acceptance as a consultative supporting teacher working as a team member with specialist colleagues'.

Another factor which facilitated the establishment of a wider role for heads of remedial departments was a simple one — the title by which the member of staff was known. A 'head of remedial' was expected by both staff and students to be responsible for less academically able pupils; the role of a 'learning adviser', on the other hand, was less specifically defined, making it easier for the member of staff concerned to work with subject teachers and to help a wider range of pupils with learning difficulties. A few heads of department had used in-service training to draw the attention of subject teachers to the problems faced by slow learners in ordinary classrooms, following up the initial meeting by more detailed work in specific subject areas with classroom teachers. This stresses the importance of close liaison between the teacher in charge of slow learner provision and the head, on all matters of school policy which are seen to affect slow learning pupils.

Beyond school, most heads of department contacted support agencies directly, while a few were required to make such requests through the school's senior management team. While all 791 schools in the survey called upon a range of support services as required, comments indicated that some, particularly the advisory and psychological services, appeared to be over-stretched and unable to meet all the requests made of them. Heads of department encouraged parents to visit the school informally and to take an active interest in their child's progress. Some even made home visits to contact parents who did not respond to invitations to call at the school. For older pupils, heads of department arranged link courses, work experience and community service schemes, often drawing on contacts built up over a number of years.

Heads of department thus supervised work both within and outside the school which took place in a variety of curricular areas. Several of the staff visited held other responsibilities in the school, which automatically brought them into contact with many other teachers. One, for example, was deputy head, another ran induction courses for all new staff and a third took charge of the school's audio-visual equipment. A number of heads were aware of the problem of isolation experienced by some heads of remedial department and several in the survey questioned whether a special department was the best way of organizing provision for slow learners. As one head wrote, 'Perhaps a "good" school has no staff who *specialize* in teaching slow learners. Specialist teachers and departments encourage other teachers to shrug off the problem.'

Chapter five

The Teachers

Personal qualities of sympathy, understanding and patience together with teaching ability are more important attributes for teachers of slow learners than academic qualification or previous experience. (Head of an inner city comprehensive)

All too often teachers in secondary schools are not adequately prepared to deal with slow learning pupils. Rarely does initial training prepare them for this work and more guidelines and in-service training would be enormously beneficial. (Head of suburban comprehensive)

5.1 The Teachers

In this chapter details of the training and teaching experience of those members of staff who taught slow learners in sample schools are given, together with information on the nature and scale of a teacher's present appointment. Teachers' views concerning the value of specialist training and the desirability of gaining general teaching experience before working with slow learners are explored and their membership of professional associations recorded. Information was gathered by means of a brief questionnaire which elicited a response from 442 teachers who were in charge of provision for slow learners and 1025 other members of staff. There were 465 schools represented, all of which had taken part in the initial survey. The final section of the chapter explores the availability of training courses for those who wish to teach slow learners.

Over two-thirds (68 per cent) of the teachers in the sample were women, contrasting with a national population of full-time and part-time staff teaching in secondary schools in March 1979, of whom 47 per cent were women (Statistics of Education 1979, DES). Nine per cent of the sample worked part-time, as compared with a national figure of six per cent for part-time staff in March 1979 (DES, 1979). The allocation of Scale posts for the whole sample is shown below, together with details of the distribution of such posts among full-time secondary teachers throughout England and Wales.

Percentage of Teachers in the Sample (*N*=1453)	Scale of Post	Percentage of All Secondary Staff (*N*=240,416 (DES, 1979))
43	1	32
25	2	27
21	3	21
8	4	11
3	Heads, Deputy Heads and Senior Teachers	9
100		100

Heads and senior staff are under-represented in our sample of those who taught slow learners, and scale 1 teachers over-represented as compared with national statistics. This may be partly accounted for by our inclusion of 130 part-time staff, who do not appear in the DES statistics, and partly by the fact that few heads and senior staff are involved in teaching slow learners.

Appointments Held by Teachers of Slow Learners

The type of appointment held by those who taught slow learners is shown in Table 5.1 which also gives details of the scale of each post. One hundred and fifty one members of staff held responsibilities in more than one sphere; most usually the curricular responsibility was shared with a pastoral one, but other appointments were concerned with management such as head of lower school. There were three head teachers who spent some of their time teaching slow learners.

Throughout this chapter a distinction is drawn between assistant teachers *per se* and assistant teachers who hold additional responsibilities, for example, a head of year or head of department. Half of

Table 5.1: *Appointments held by teachers of slow learners*

Type of Appointment	Scale of Post					Total	%
	1	2	3	4	Senior Teacher		
Assistant teacher	546	182	12	–	–	740	(51)
Assistant teacher with other duties	25	13	8	6	35	87†	(6)
Head of department	21	68	198	76	3	366	(25)
Head of department plus other duties	2	6	35	8	4	55	(4)
Teacher in charge of subject or of slow learners	20	66	25	6	2	119	(8)
Year head	5	9	27	10	4	55	(4)
House head	3	10	4	5	–	22	(2)
Teachers with other combinations of responsibilities	1	2	2	1	3‡	9	(neg)
	623	356	311	112	51	1453	(100)

Note: † Other duties, e.g. head of lower school, counsellor.

‡ Three heads taught slow learners.

No response – 14.

those in the sample (51 per cent) were assistant teachers without other specific responsibilities, appointed on scales 1 to 3, and a further six per cent, appointed on scales ranging from 1 to senior teacher, had additional specific responsibilities. Four hundred and twenty one (29 per cent) were heads of subject or remedial departments on scales ranging from 1 to 5, some of whom also held other responsibilities. One hundred and nineteen members of staff (8 per cent) were in charge of a subject area or of the provision made for slow learning pupils but did not necessarily hold a scale post for this. Teachers with other kinds of specific responsibilities such as school counsellor, teacher in charge of careers, the library or of the 6th form, year head, house head, or deputy head constituted 6 per cent of the sample. From examining the more detailed records of time per week spent teaching slow learners, it was evident that heads of subject departments, year heads and many of those designated senior teachers spent less than one-quarter of their teaching time with slow learners, as other commitments intervened.

A separate analysis was made of those teachers who were responsible for organizing the provision for slow learners in their respective schools. Details appear in Table 5.2, which shows that 75 per cent (330) were heads of a special slow learner department, 15 per cent (63) were designated 'teacher in charge of slow learner provision' and 10 per cent (47) were assistant teachers with no official title but who were known to be the reference point for consultation and discussion about slow learner provision.

Table 5.2: *Appointments held by teachers with responsibility for slow learner provision.*

Type of Appointment	Number and Percentage of Teachers					
	Middle Schools $N=49$		Other Secondary $N=391$		Total $N=440$	
	N	%	N	%	N	%
Assistant teacher	17	(35)	15	(4)	32	(7)
Assistant with other duties	–	–	15	(4)	15	(3)
Head of department	17	(35)	272	(70)	289	(66)
Head of department plus other duties	1	(2)	40	(10)	41	(9)
In charge of slow learner provision	14	(28)	45	(11)	59	(14)
In charge of slow learner provision plus other duties	–	–	4	(1)	4	(1)
	49	(100)	391	(100)	440	(100)

No response – 2.

When these data are viewed separately for middle and for other secondary schools, the following pattern of appointments emerges, as shown in Table 5.2. Although the numbers are small and should be interpreted with caution, it appears that in middle schools more assistant teacher posts are likely to carry responsibility for slow learner provision than in other secondary schools. As a result, only 37 per cent of middle schools had a head of department whereas 80 per cent of those with responsibility for slow learner provision in other secondary schools were heads of special remedial departments.

Teaching Experience

Teaching experience as shown in Appendix 5A.1 was extremely varied. Almost half (48 per cent) of those surveyed had experience of the secondary sector only, a small number (6 per cent) had taught in junior and middle schools while over one-third (36 per cent) had teaching experience which extended into both primary and secondary sectors. A few teachers, representing approximately ten per cent of the sample, had a variety of other kinds of teaching experience: teaching infants, teaching in the independent sector or in forces schools overseas, for example. Eleven per cent of all the staff who answered the questionnaire had taught in special schools. These included ESN(M) and ESN(S) schools, units and schools for the physically handicapped, partially hearing and partially sighted, as well as for pupils with behaviour or maladjustment problems. Most of these were all-age establishments.

An important related issue concerned the training of staff who taught slow learners. Was initial training or was general teaching experience plus in-service training the most suitable preparation for those who wished to teach slow learning pupils? To gauge the opinion of teachers who had between them a wide range of educational experience, a variety of different kinds of training and who had started teaching slow learners at different times in their careers, the following question was posed:

> What are your views on the suggestion that teachers should have general teaching experience before specializing in teaching slow learners?

Teachers were provided with five alternative answers on a scale ranging from 'essential' to 'irrelevant', and responses were as follows:

The Importance of General Teaching Experience	Percentage $N=1437$
Essential	39
Very important	43
Not very important	14
Not necessary at all	3
Irrelevant as teachers should not specialise in teaching slow learners	1

Thus 82 per cent of teachers in the sample were convinced of the importance of gaining general teaching experience before teaching slow learners, 14 per cent did not consider this to be particularly important and four per cent stated that there was no necessity to gain additional teaching experience.

5.2 Subjects Taught to Slow Learners

Teachers were asked 'Which subject do you spend *most* of your time teaching to slow learners?' and their responses are tabulated in Table 5.3. Not surprisingly, by far the greatest number of staff, 74 per cent, devoted most or all of their time to the teaching of basic skills, i.e. literacy and numeracy. Fifty per cent of all the teachers in the

Table 5.3: *Subjects on which the majority of teaching time with slow learners was spent*

Subjects	Heads of Remedial Departments/Teachers in Charge of Slow Learner Provision N=438		Other Teachers N=1020		Total Staff N=1458	
		%		%		%
English/literacy skills	267	(61)	469	(46)	736	(50)
Maths/numeracy skills	27	(6)	152	(15)	179	(12)
Literacy and numeracy skills	69	(16)	99	(10)	168	(12)
Science	1	(neg.)	21	(2)	22	(2)
Humanities including English	9	(2)	56	(6)	65	(5)
Humanities excluding English	4	(1)	31	(2)	35	(2)
General Subjects	6	(2)	48	(5)	54	(4)
Practical subjects e.g. craft	1	(neg.)	18	(2)	19	(1)
Other subjects	54	(12)	126	(100)	180	(12)
	438	(100)	1020	(100)	1458	(100)

No response – 9 (Heads of Departments 4, Teachers 5).

survey spent most of their time teaching literacy skills alone, 12 per cent taught mainly numeracy skills while a further 12 per cent were equally involved in teaching both of these basic skills to slow learners. An additional five per cent of the staff taught mainly English and humanities while a further four per cent taught general subjects which commonly included elements of literacy, numeracy, humanities and a craft or science subject. Thus a total of 83 per cent of the teachers surveyed spent most of their time teaching basic skills to slow learners, while a minority taught mainly science (2 per cent), humanities (2 per cent) or craft (1 per cent). The remaining 12 per cent of teachers provided slow learners with a wide variety of experiences which included music, French conversation, typing, careers education, horticulture, economics, dance and childcare. In a small number of schools, 4th and 5th year slow learners were given the opportunity to take part in other special activities which included community service, the Schools' Traffic Education Programme (STEP) and the Record of Personal Achievement Scheme. For each of these there was one member of staff responsible for preparing and implementing the programmes.

As outlined in Chapter four, while the majority of schools made provision for slow learners within a special department, others appointed one or more staff who taught slow learners but who did not constitute a separate department. Some made use of the local authority's peripatetic remedial service and in others heads of department were given the responsibility of catering for slow learning pupils within their subject area. The teacher questionnaires could therefore be grouped into four categories. First, members of a remedial department (75 per cent of the teachers in the survey); second, those appointed to teach slow learners but who did not constitute a department (nine per cent); third, faculty or departmental staff who had responsibility for slow learner provision specifically within their own subject areas (four per cent); and fourth, other members of the staff who spent some of their time teaching slow learners each week (12 per cent).

Analysis revealed that four out of five remedial staff taught the basic skills of English or maths compared with only one in two of the subject teachers. As expected, science, humanities, PE, practical and craft subjects were more often taught to slow learners by subject specialists than by remedial teachers. The data also showed that 67 per cent of remedial department staff and 48 per cent of other remedial teachers spent either no time at all or less than 3½ hours per week teaching pupils other than slow learners while only 12 per cent of subject teachers had timetables primarily devoted to slow learner groups.

5.3 Teacher Training

While 97 per cent of the teachers (1429/1457) had received initial training, in less than one-third of these cases (30 per cent) had the training included a component on the education of slow learners. Appendix 5A.2 gives details of the age groups for which teachers were trained and also indicates which courses contained a unit on slow learners.

Seventy-one per cent of those with teacher training were prepared for teaching in middle and/or secondary schools (1014/1420); of these, fewer than one-third had taken a course which included a component relating to slow learners. Twenty-three per cent had trained for infant or junior age groups, (322/1420) and fewer than one-third of these had followed a course on slow learners. The remaining six per cent of teachers had taken other training courses and just over one-third reported that a component on slow learners had been included.

When training for the different sections is viewed without the inclusion of those staff whose courses catered for more than one age group, differences appear which deserve mention. Twenty-five per cent of those with secondary training alone had taken a course on slow learners, compared with 33 per cent of those prepared for junior teaching and 46 per cent of those who were trained to teach in middle schools. When information on slow learner training is related

Number of Years Since Completing Training	Percentage of Teachers with Slow Learner Component in Training
Up to 5	54
6–10	33
11–15	19
16–20	14
21–25	14
Over 25	11

to the number of years a member of staff has taught, it would appear that the availability and take-up of special courses or course components concerned with slow learners in initial training has increased in the last decade, and particularly so since the mid 1970s. These data were provided by 867 members of staff whose teaching careers had been continuous.

Specialist Training

Over eighty per cent of teachers considered that it was essential or very important to have special training for teaching slow learners, a sentiment expressed equally strongly by those with special training as well as by those without. (Appendix 5A.3)

When head teachers were asked what they considered to be important when selecting staff who were to teach slow learners for some or all of the time, 70 per cent included 'formal qualifications' in the teaching of slow learners in their answer. Thus the consensus of opinion among both heads and their staffs was in favour of those who taught slow learners having special training, either initial or in-service, for their work with these pupils.

5.4 Qualifications Held by Teachers of Slow Learners

Table 5.4 illustrates the different kinds of qualification held by those who taught slow learners. Seventy-two per cent of the staff held Certificates of Education from one-, two- or three-year college of education courses. Some of these teachers, representing sixteen per cent of the sample, had subsequently taken diplomas and certificates, many of which were in remedial or special education. Eight per cent of the sample had followed the Certificate by a degree and are therefore included in the graduate statistics which follow. Eleven per cent held a B.Ed. Degree and over half of these had preceded this by a Certificate of Education. A total of 13 per cent held B.A., B.Com. or B.Sc. degrees and of these almost three-quarters had entered teaching after taking a one year postgraduate certificate in education (PGCE). The one per cent with higher degrees comprised 20 staff with masters degrees and one teacher with a doctorate. Among the

Table 5.4: *Qualifications held by teachers of slow learners*

	Teachers in Charge of Provision for Slow Learners		Other Staff		All Teachers	
	$N=396$	%	$N=946$	%	$N=1342$	%
Cert.Ed. only	192	(49)	548	(59)	740	(56)
Cert.Ed. + B.Ed.	17	(4)	54	(6)	71	(5)
Cert.Ed. + B.A./B.Sc.	12	(3)	33	(3)	45	(3)
Cert.Ed. + other diplomas and certificates	113	(28)	99	(10)	212	(16)
B.Ed. only	16	(4)	66	(7)	82	(6)
B.A./B.Sc. + PGCE	15	(4)	94	(10)	109	(8)
B.A./B.Sc. + PGCE +other diplomas and certificates	7	(2)	4	(neg.)	11	(1)
B.A./B.Sc. + other diplomas and certificates	4	(1)	11	(1)	15	(1)
Other types and groups of qualifications	14	(4)	22	(3)	36	(3)
M.A./M.Sc./M.Ed./Ph.D.	6	(1)	15	(1)	21	(1)
	396	(100)	946	(100)	1342	(100)

No response–125. (Teachers in Charge of Provision 46, Teachers 79).

three per cent of teachers holding other types and combinations of qualifications, half were graduates.

Thus 72 per cent of the staff were non-graduate certificated teachers, 27 per cent were graduates and one per cent held other qualifications in art, dance, drama, technology, music, PE and counselling. The major difference found between heads of department and other staff was that 30 per cent of those in charge of slow learner provision had followed their initial degree or certificate by obtaining further qualifications in special or remedial education, compared with only ten per cent of others who taught slow learners.

5.5 Subject Background

Over 800 teachers, repesenting 56 per cent of the sample, provided details of the main subjects which they had studied during their certificate, diploma or degree course.

As shown by Table 5.5, almost one-quarter of the staff were

Table 5.5: *Main subjects studied by teachers of slow learners*

Main Subject	No. of Teachers ($N=814$)	%
English	178	(22)
Geography	82	(10)
History	82	(10)
Science	66	(8)
Maths	63	(8)
PE	62	(8)
Art, Craft, Design	52	(6)
RE	35	(4)
General Subjects	31	(4)
Music	18	(2)
Psychology	18	(2)
Education	17	(2)
Modern Languages	16	(2)
Humanities/Social Studies	15	(2)
Sociology	13	(2)
Home Economics	12	(1)
Special Education	9	(1)
Other subjects, e.g. Drama, Economics, Commerce, Geology, Classics	45	(6)
	814	(100)

qualified in English (22 per cent) and a further quarter in the humanities areas of geography, history, RE, sociology and social studies (28 per cent). One-sixth had qualified in maths or science (16 per cent) and a similar number in the creative and practical subjects of art, craft, music, design, home economics and PE (17 per cent).

The remaining 17 per cent of those who taught slow learners were qualified in a variety of different subjects.

The data were analysed separately for graduate and for non-graduate staff. Almost 300 of the 367 graduates provided details of their subject backgrounds. Appendix 5A.4 shows that one-fifth were English graduates (20 per cent), one-quarter had read the humanities subjects of history, geography, social studies or RE (25 per cent) and a further nine per cent had studied psychology or sociology. Thus over half of the graduate staff had backgrounds in English or the social or behavioural sciences, only one-seventh had taken maths or science degrees (14 per cent) and the creative and practical subjects were repesented by a mere four per cent of graduate staff. The remaining one-quarter had read for a variety of subjects which included education (6 per cent), economics (2 per cent), special education (3 per cent), modern languages (5 per cent) and general subjects (3 per cent), as well as smaller numbers of staff whose disciplines included politics, geology, classics, drama and technology.

Five hundred and sixteen of the 952 non-graduate certificated teachers provided details of the main subjects which they had studied during training. A number of responses indicated that two subjects had been studied. Where these were given equal status, e.g. English and history, they appear on the table as 'English + one other subject'. The response for 'History and English', however, is recorded elsewhere in the table, the initial subject area being given priority.

The analysis in Appendix 5A.5 shows that approximately one-quarter of the certificated teachers had taken English as a main subject (23 per cent), one-quarter were qualified in the humanities, i.e. history, geography or RE (25 per cent) and one-quarter had a background in creative or practical subjects, i.e. art, craft, wood-work, metalwork, home economics, design, PE or music (26 per cent). Less than one-fifth of the teachers had qualified to teach maths or science subjects (18 per cent), and very few had studied general subjects. Eight per cent of staff had studied other subjects such as sociology, drama, economics or general subjects.

Thus both graduate and non-graduate staff groups contained similar percentages of teachers with backgrounds in English, humanities, maths and the sciences, but widely differing percentages of those who had studied creative or practical subjects, languages, special education and the social sciences.

5.6 In-Service Training

During the preceding five years, a total of 774 teachers in the survey had attended in-service courses concerned with teaching slow learners. This represented 53 per cent of the sample. A difference in the rates of participation between heads of remedial departments and other staff members was noted, since 83 per cent of those in charge of slow learner provision had taken part in in-service courses as compared with 40 per cent of other teachers.

All staff were asked to record the course title or subject and to give names of sponsors with details of the length of each course and the pattern of attendance required: in this case, full-time or part-time. Details of any qualifications gained by this means were requested and teachers were asked to indicate which aspects of the courses had proved most helpful to their teaching.

A total of 1407 courses was recorded, 59 per cent of which were concerned specifically with remedial education and seven per cent of which focused on special education. The remaining 34 per cent of courses contained elements relating to the teaching of slow learners but were not solely concerned with this topic. Courses on handwriting or on the teaching of reading, for example, were included in the responses to this question. Of the courses attended, 70 per cent were organized by the local education authority, ten per cent were run by the DES, two per cent were provided by NARE and 18 per cent had other sponsors such as university departments of education, colleges of education or the College of Preceptors.

Table 5.6 gives details of the balance of full-time, part-time and short courses attended, shown separately for heads of departments and for other teachers. The full-time courses comprised mainly one year degree, certificate and diploma courses but also included a number of three, four and six week courses. Chief providers were the DES and local education authorities. It should be remembered in this context that for one year courses secondment was usually a financial prerequisite. Part-time courses, which varied widely in nature and in length, included non-certificated evening courses as well as certificated courses which extended over a year or more. Most short courses were of one, two or five days' duration, while a few, such as University Summer Schools, extended over two weeks.

One hundred and forty seven of the 774 teachers had acquired additional qualifications by attending in-service training courses,

Table 5.6: *Attendance at in-service courses*

	Heads of Remedial Departments N=442		Other Teachers of Slow Learners N=1025		Total Staff 1467	
	N	(%)	N	(%)	N	(%)
Full-time courses only (over 3 weeks duration)	113	(26)	102	(10)	211	(15)
Part-time or short courses only†	212	(48)	291	(29)	511	(35)
Both full-time and part-time/ short courses	37	(8)	12	(1)	45	(3)
No course details given	3	(1)	4	(neg.)	7	(neg.)
No courses attended	77	(17)	616	(60)	693	(47)
	442	(100)	1025	(100)	1467	(100)

† Short courses comprise those of two weeks' duration or less and include many two day and five day (one week) courses. There were no recorded courses which extended beyond two weeks and yet less than three.

representing 19 per cent of all who took courses concerned with the teaching of slow learners. Examples of qualifications gained by this means included the Diploma in Education, the Diploma in Reading Development, the Advanced Certificate in Special Education, the Diploma in Special Education and the Diploma in Counselling. A number of staff gained qualifications from the College of Preceptors, some acquired a certificate in Further Professional Studies and a few took the Diploma in Advanced Study in Education. Many teachers had acquired other diplomas and certificates concerned with remedial or special education, on courses which ranged in length from one term to three years. Twenty-two per cent of heads of department and those in charge of slow learner provision who attended courses gained qualifications in this way as compared with 16 per cent of other staff.

Those aspects of the courses which teachers found particularly helpful are recorded in Table 5.7. By far the most important aspect cited was the opportunity to meet with other teachers of slow learners; to exchange ideas and to hold discussions on topics of mutual concern was seen to be particularly helpful by 43 per cent of those who completed this section of the questionnaire. 'Moral support in a largely undervalued area of teaching' was one quotation which summed up the feelings of many teachers on this issue.

Table 5.7: *Aspects of in-service courses considered to be most valuable by teachers of slow learners*

Aspects of Course	N=634†	% of Course Members Responding to Question
Discussion with other teachers of slow learners	273	43
Opportunity to see/use new books, equipment and resources	153	24
Practical guidance on teaching methods	90	14
Testing and diagnostic measures for the assessment of learning difficulty	81	13
Language development/teaching of reading	68	11
Visits to other schools, both special and ordinary	47	7
Keeping up to date with reading and research	42	7
Subject specific issues	38	6
'All aspects helpful'	18	3
No part of course helpful	16	3

† 140 course members made no response to this question, and many considered more than one aspect to be valuable.

Displays of new books, equipment and teaching materials were viewed by 24 per cent of respondents as helpful to their teaching and many went on to explain that this was one way of finding out about newly published materials and of having the chance not only to see them but on occasion to borrow items for classroom use. Several staff mentioned that it had been useful to watch demonstrations of new materials and equipment.

The third most helpful aspect of many courses was seen to be the practical guidance which was given on teaching methods via workshop sessions, through discussion or by means of more formal lectures. Twenty-one per cent of course members felt that practical guidance on teaching techniques and classroom management and/or the opportunity to see others teaching in a range of different environments in both special and ordinary schools were particularly helpful aspects of in-service courses.

Thirteen per cent of responses concerned testing and the use of diagnostic measures for the assessment of learning difficuty; eleven per cent were focused on the teaching of reading and on language development while smaller numbers related to other aspects of courses which teachers perceived as helpful. For example, some felt that in-service training provided a valuable 'breathing space' and the opportunity to keep up-to-date with research developments; others welcomed the chance to step outside the classroom for a period and to 'stand back and gain objectivity', while others were glad to learn more about the work of the support services and in particular, the role of the educational psychologist. Several staff recorded that in-service courses had given them more confidence in assessing the needs of pupils at different stages of development and had consequently proved helpful to their lesson planning and in the construction of suitable remedial programmes. Of the few who had found a subject-specific topic particularly useful, half had attended courses focused on the teaching of mathematics to slow learners.

Many other topics were mentioned reflecting the variety and nature of the courses attended by teachers in the survey. Courses involving a study of maladjustment and dyslexia, multicultural education, text readability, running a department, record keeping, handwriting, counselling, study skills and the teaching of spelling were all deemed helpful. As one teacher explained, in-service courses provided 'a touchstone, a reference to outside school' which was perceived as a particularly valuable aspect by many course participants.

5.7 Membership of Professional Associations Concerned with Slow Learners

Twenty-four per cent of those in the survey belonged to associations which were concerned in some way with slow learning pupils. Teachers in charge of slow learner provision were more often members of such associations than were their colleagues; fifty per cent of the heads of department recorded membership as compared with 13 per cent of other staff. The range of associations was small, and the major groups mentioned are listed below, together with the percentage of the sample who registered membership. As one-fifth of all teachers belonged to two or three associations, the percentages do not add up to 100.

Name of Association Concerned with Slow Learners	*% of Teachers Recording Membership (N=354)*
National Association for Remedial Education (NARE)	82
United Kingdom Reading Association (UKRA)	18
National Council for Special Education (NCSE)	6
Local Associations (Remedial Education)	7
Local Associations (Dyslexia)	2

Other associations mentioned included the Association for Workers for Maladjusted Children, local branches of the National Council for Special Education, (NCSE), the National Association for Teachers of English (NATE) and the National Association for Multiracial Education (NAME).

5.8 Further Issues

Five hundred and seventy teachers responded to the invitation to comment on issues which they felt should be considered in the context of the research. The greatest number of points made centred on training, both initial and in-service, for teaching slow learners. Thirty-eight per cent of those who replied to the question expressed concern over the fact that few initial and in-service courses concerned with remedial education were currently available. As one teacher explained:

> All too often, teachers are not adequately prepared in secondary schools to deal with slow learning pupils. Initial training frequently does not prepare them for this work. Guidelines and in-service training would be enormously beneficial.

This member of staff also maintained that no initial training course for secondary teaching should omit a section on work with slow learners, since 'there is no area of the curriculum where a teacher does not come into contact with pupils with learning difficulties'. Another teacher stressed that students should be in regular contact with slow learners during initial training and several questioned the advisability of staff in their first year of service teaching classes of slow learning pupils. It was suggested that probationers might teach small groups or individuals, or work as part of a team of teachers to gain experience. However, slightly different views were put by seven per cent of the teachers, who felt that while training might be helpful, a teacher's temperament, personality and above all, *wish* to teach slow learners was of paramount importance. Qualities such as patience, sympathy, empathy, interest and understanding were frequently quoted as desirable attributes.

The role of the remedial teacher was seen to be an important issue by nine per cent of respondents, many of whom stressed the necessity of making time to fulfil the pastoral and counselling responsibilities which they saw as central to their work. Almost half of those concerned with the role of the remedial teacher felt that remedial staff should also teach some mainstream pupils (63 per cent of the teachers in the sample did so) 'to retain a total perspective of the school'. Other aspects mentioned included the balance of time spent with slow learners with other pupils during the school week, and the advisory role of such a teacher or team of teachers. A wider role than that traditionally found in schools was sought by many and seen to be 'important for the status and well-being of the teachers as well as for the children'. Eleven per cent of teachers surveyed considered that there should be more liaison between teachers of slow learners and other staff and between remedial departments and subject departments. A number also commented on the value to be gained from liaising with parents and with the support services beyond school as well as with primary and middle feeder schools.

The question of departmental and of personal status in schools was raised by ten per cent of respondents. Several felt that remedial work was still a 'Cinderella subject' and many considered that career prospects were poor. (The survey revealed that most (55 per cent) of the heads of department were on scale 3, 17 per cent were on scale 4 and 2 per cent on the Senior Teacher Scale.) Organization and grouping procedures were felt by ten per cent of respondents to be an important issue where slow learners were concerned. The balance of lessons between the slow learner department and the mainstream, the degree of integration with other pupils, the size of the group(s) in which slow learners were taught, the structure of the teaching group and the range of ability within it were the most commonly quoted items of concern to teachers. Eight per cent of teachers raised questions concerning the identification of the 'slow learners' and more specifically about the detection and causes of learning difficulties and the implications that this might have on subsequent provision and teaching strategies. As one head of department explained:

> We should look at the areas in which they fail, rather than at the failing pupils themselves, as we need to question whether 'remedial' pupils are a population distinct from others, or whether their performance merely underlines inadequacies in our teaching, in spite of which their schoolmates succeed.

Curricular issues all centred on the necessity of establishing course aims and content objectives for slow learning pupils within the framework of a curriculum which was planned as a whole. Nine per cent of teachers were concerned to see that slow learners in all year groups were given an appropriate curriculum.

Other issues included the scarcity of resource materials suitable for use with slow learners, especially in mainstream classes, the importance of preserving adequate provision for slow learners in the face of the current staffing reductions, the maintenance of good communication within a large remedial department and the question of whether a departmental structure was really the most appropriate way of catering for slow learners. There were pleas for improved staffing ratios to permit some work to take place on a one-to-one basis. In this context, a few highlighted the special problems faced by small schools in which the present staffing establishment precluded the individual teaching of slow learning pupils. Some teachers saw a need for the provision of more vocational 4th and 5th year courses and for increased liaison on behalf of this age group to take place with employers, with a view to establishing more work experience opportunities for slow learners.

Two further issues of a more peripheral nature deserve comment. The first concerned the primary sector, in which four per cent of teachers felt more work with slow learners should be undertaken in the way of identification and special provision for slow learning pupils. 'Early diagnosis and treatment is essential before apathy and lack of self-confidence develops' was one comment which expressed the views of most on this issue. The second area, mentioned by only one per cent, concerned those pupils who were just outside the group identified as 'slow learners' and who were often found in the next band, stream or set to the slow learner group or were less readily identifiable as a group in mixed ability classes. As one head of department explained, this was 'the twilight area' in which were a number of pupils who required help but not a full programme of remedial education; how best to provide for their needs was a problem.

5.9 Training to Teach Slow Learners

The final section of this chapter outlines the findings of a survey of teacher training, which took place during the early months of the project. Information was gathered about complete courses as well as those which contained a component on slow learners. The purpose of the survey was to explore the nature, availability and take-up of such courses for teachers of slow learning pupils.

Difficulties were encountered in locating courses and it is anticipated that potential applicants would encounter similar problems. *The Handbook of Institutions 1978/79* published by NATFHE and *The Programme of Long Courses for Qualified Teachers* and *Short Courses 1978/79* published by the Department of Education and Science were used in an attempt to locate both initial and in-service training courses. Information concerning relevant courses was requested from all universities with education departments and colleges of education and polytechnics which offered initial teacher training. Enquiry slips were also sent to every college and polytechnic listed in the handbooks as running in-service courses on slow learners.

From these procedures 214 courses were identified, some of which were wholly concerned with the slow learner and others with components which were relevant to the education of slow learners. Forty-four of the courses led to a postgraduate certificate in education (PGCE), 92 were part of initial training programmes leading to a B.Ed. degree or Certificate in Education (Cert.Ed.) and 78 were in-service courses. Questionnaires were sent to the tutors of the 214 courses identified, and 107 were returned. Details were therefore on file for 20 PGCE courses, 40 Certificate in Education (Cert.Ed.) or B.Ed. degree courses and 47 in-service courses, some of which led to diplomas and certificates.

Initial Training Courses

Only five of the 20 PGCE courses for which information was received offered the teaching of slow learners as a main unit of study and in a further 13 the education of slow learners was available as a subsidiary option. Of the 40 courses leading to Cert.Ed. or B.Ed., two were options which could be chosen as a second subject, 25 offered a component on slow learners as a supplementary option and 12 included units on slow learners as part of the compulsory core. One was a 'topping up' course designed to consolidate special education units which were part of a Diploma in Higher Education.

Entry to many of these courses was restricted. Applicants with a psychology or social science degree and experience of working with children were those most likely to be accepted for the PGCE courses. Where a slow learner option in a B.Ed./Cert.Ed. course was available as a second subject, this was not introduced until the third or fourth year and a limited number of students from those already involved in the training course were selected. For some options, entry was restricted to certain groups of students, for example those training to teach in secondary and middle schools, B.Ed. students or those who had completed prerequisite units.

The number of applicants exceeded the number of places available on all major and second subject courses. For the five major PGCE courses in 1978, 148 applications were made for 65 places and 72 students were finally accepted. Similarly, some of the options on PGCE and Cert. Ed. or B.Ed. courses were over-subscribed by 20 or more applications. In some institutions, students were selected to fill the limited number of places available; in others it was policy to try to accommodate all who wished to participate.

Course length and the total number of teaching hours provided were found to vary considerably. The duration of that part of the programme which related to slow learner education varied from one week to over three terms, and the total teaching time on the subject of slow learner education ranged from under 30 hours to over 150 hours. As expected, the PGCE main and B.Ed. second subject courses allocated most teaching time to slow learners, while almost half of the optional units contained less than 30 hours tuition time.

Two-thirds of all the initial training courses featured block placements as an integral part of the programme. These, which generally comprised two seven-week periods of teaching practice, on which up to half of the time was spent with slow learners, were included in all major slow learner courses. Postgraduate courses also included visits to special schools, assessment centres, child guidance clinics and the schools' psychological service. Many of the other courses included some opportunity for teaching slow learners, usually by means of a series of short visits. For example, in one institution where slow learner education was available as a second subject to the main field of study, students spent one morning per week for four weeks in the same school, assessing pupils' needs and planning and teaching an appropriate remedial programme. On other courses, visits varied from those occasionally organized for individual students on a voluntary basis to a programme of ten half-day visits to schools and clinics. One-third of the initial training courses identified did not include any placements or visits associated with slow learner education.

These initial certificate, degree and post-graduate training courses were designed for three groups of teachers: for those wishing to specialize in remedial or special education; for those wishing to offer remedial teaching as a subsidiary subject; and for subject specialists who wanted to broaden their knowledge of the needs of pupils with learning difficulties in the ordinary classroom. In a few cases the courses were also recommended for those who planned to become educational psychologists after a period of teaching. Major topics in initial courses included the teaching of language and literacy skills, testing procedures, the identification of the child with learning problems, the causes of learning difficulty and the organization of special provision for slow learners in ordinary schools. Full details are given in Table 5.8. Other topics offered by some institutions included the use and evaluation of resource materials, the teaching of maths, the use of support services, record keeping and a study of teaching methods appropriate for pupils with learning difficulties.

Table 5.8: *Course content: components listed by tutors*

	Initial Courses N=60	In-service Courses N=43	All N=103
Testing/Assessment/Diagnosis of learning difficulties	36	29	65
Identifying the child with learning difficulties	29	17	46
Causes/Aetiology of learning difficulties	27	15	42
Teaching methods	20	21	41
Teaching of: reading	26	19	45
literacy/writing/spelling/ language	15	25	40
basic skills	3	10	13
numeracy	15	24	39
Language development	5	10	15
Curriculum design/development	14	24	38
Use/evaluation of teaching materials	12	11	23
Organization of provision for slow learners	37	17	54
Special education	23	26	49
Implications of the Warnock Report	18	20	38
Behaviour/maladjustment problems	15	18	33
Psychology	6	25	31
Use of educational agencies	18	10	28
Child development	5	16	21
Sociology	2	14	16
Home/family background	4	8	12
Multicultural education	3	6	9
Counselling/welfare/pastoral work	1	6	7
Educational research methods	–	7	7
Other topics	24	29	53
	374	450	824

In-service Courses

Seventy-eight in-service courses were located from the DES and NATFHE handbooks and from enquiries to universities and colleges of education which appeared to provide courses for serving teachers. Courses organized by local education authorities or teachers' centres were not included in this survey as these are not advertised nationally and are usually available only to teachers within the area. With very few exceptions, the in-service courses identified were located in large urban or metropolitan centres such as London, Birmingham, Newcastle, Bristol, Southampton and Swansea, creating obvious difficulties for teachers who did not live or work in the larger centres of population.

Information was received from 47 of the in-service courses; six of which led to higher degree, ten to a B.Ed. degree, 25 to a certificate or diploma of education and six of which did not result in any award. The requirements for admission to all in-service courses were a teacher's certificate plus two, or in some cases, up to five years of teaching experience. For the higher degree courses, a first degree, an advanced diploma or its equivalent was desirable, experience in teaching slow learners was sought and LEA support was an additional financial prerequisite for many intending students.

In-service courses leading to recognized awards were generally longer than those for which no award was given. For example, most of the higher degree courses took two years to complete, the duration of a B.Ed. degree was between one and three years, depending on the student's previous qualification and most diploma courses were designed to be completed in one year. In contrast, courses which were not award-bearing were all between one and four terms in length. Twenty-three of the 47 courses were full-time, with or without a part-time commitment, 20 courses were part-time only, with attendance once or twice a week, either during the day or evening and sometimes at weekends. Four courses could be attended part-time or full-time. Details appear in Table 5.9. Visits and placements were organized on 35 of the 47 in-service courses, but on part-time courses visits were not always feasible.

For most courses the number of applicants exceeded the number of places available. The six courses leading to a higher degree, for example, received 383 applications for 107 places and 103 students were finally accepted. There were 105 applicants for 15 places on one diploma course and 50 students were finally admitted. In contrast, one of the B.Ed. courses was under-subscribed, as only seven applications were received for 12 places. Several courses which received many applications opened with places still unfilled; a situation which could have been caused by difficulties in obtaining secondment. The dilemma was summed up as follows by a tutor:

To me, the *key* issue is whether the DES want teachers trained for working with children with problems or not! On the one hand, we have Warnock and lip-service to the needs of children, while on the other we have absolute embargoes on full-time secondment and immense difficuties put in the way of part-time students. We have the DES begging or instructing us to set up these opportunities, while at the same time sternly talking about the 'viability' of small courses and staff-student ratios. We waste hours and hours interviewing excellent, interested candidates who have not a chance of getting secondments, and frequently have to advise people not to apply.

Table 5.9: *In-service courses: full-time and part-time elements*

Type of Course	Part-time Only	Full-time Only	Full-time + Part-time	Part-time or Full-time	No. of Courses
Higher degree	2	–	4	–	6
B.Ed.	6	–	4	–	10
Cert. or Dip.	11	9	2	3	25
No award	1	3	1	1	6
	20	12	11	4	47

Financial support and co-operation from the local education authority was necessary for most teachers wishing to attend full-time courses. A few teachers accepted places without secondment, but for many this was not a viable alternative. It is possible that some teachers did not take up places on courses because they could not obtain financial support. One tutor felt that many of the students who were currently applying for admission to part-time courses were would-be full-time applicants without secondment who preferred taking a part-time course to waiting a year or more in the hope of gaining secondment.

In-service courses, which included some higher degrees as well as degree, diploma, and non-award-bearing courses, catered for students from a variety of educational backgrounds with different kinds of teaching experience. Courses for teachers in special and in ordinary schools were available, designed for both primary and secondary age ranges. Curriculum issues dominated, as Table 5.8 shows, with the B.Ed. and the shorter one-term courses accounting for most of the subject-specific topics which appear in the Table. Many courses included several related subjects, such as science plus environmental science, art, music and drama, PE and movement. Teaching methods were commonly included in these courses. The teaching of reading was treated separately from other literacy skills such as writing, spelling and language development.

In comparison with initial courses, a higher proportion of the in-service courses offered psychology, child development, behaviour studies, sociology, special education, teaching methods for slow learners and, as stated above, units on curriculum development. Relatively fewer in-service courses were available on the causes of learning difficulty, on the organization of provision or on specific issues such as dyslexia. Any attempt to draw major conclusions from this brief survey of course content should take account of the words of one tutor who estimated that even in a densely populated urban area the teacher 'pool' from which potential members came would support an in-service course on a given topic for a maximum of five years. It is unlikely, therefore, that the courses recorded here during the 1978/79 academic year would contain the same pattern of topics in succeeding years.

5.10 Discussion

In this chapter the training, educational background and teaching experience of those staff members who taught slow learning pupils in sample schools have been explored and presented, together with information on the nature and scale of teachers' appointments and their views on the desirability of special training for work with slow learners. The availability and take-up of initial and in-service courses by those wishing to teach slow learners has been investigated and so also have teachers' opinions on the value of such training as well as on wider educational issues.

The research showed that fewer than one in three of the staff had received initial training in teaching slow learners although four out of five considered this to be an essential or very important prerequisite, as did seven out of ten heads. However, since the mid-

1970s more initial courses have incorporated a unit or units in the teaching of slow learners and over half of the staff who trained since 1975 had followed a course on slow learners, in contrast to one-fifth of those who trained ten years earlier. At present, more of this training appears to be available in courses preparing teachers for junior and/or middle school work than for secondary teaching.

As expected, most staff who taught slow learners had moved into the work from a variety of different curricular areas. However, although four out of five spent most of their time teaching the basic skills of language and number to slow learning pupils, only one in five was trained in English and one in twelve in maths. One-quarter of all staff who taught slow learners had backgrounds in the humanities subjects. This situation highlights the importance of in-service training. Indeed, over half of the staff surveyed had attended an in-service course concerned with slow learners during the preceding five years. Eighty-three per cent of teachers in charge of slow learner provision had attended at least one such course and of these, more than one in five had gained additional qualifications by this means. Other staff, too, had found in-service courses helpful; forty per cent had participated and, of these, one in six had gained further qualifications.

In-service courses were deemed particularly valuable on a number of counts. Teachers appreciated the opportunity they afforded for informal discussion, for the chance to see and to use new books and resources and to learn about practical teaching strategies. With regard to subject-specific items, language, literacy and maths were the curricular areas most frequently mentioned as being particularly helpful. Most of these in-service courses were arranged by the LEAs, whose role in the professional development of staff was found to be particularly important in areas outside the major metropolitan and city zones. Most courses on slow learners listed in the DES and NATFHE handbooks were organized in the larger centres of population, leaving teachers living and working elsewhere almost totally reliant on the LEAs for in-service opportunities and also as a source of financial support for those wishing to undertake full-time further study. The in-service courses surveyed were found to contain more units on language development and the teaching of reading and numeracy than did initial courses; similarly curriculum development, psychology and behavioural problems were more frequently addressed in an in-service than an initial training course.

The national survey of initial courses identified from the DES and NATFHE handbooks indicated that all the major courses were over-subscribed and revealed that their major focus appeared to be on assessment, testing, the causes of learning difficulty and methods of identifying and making provision for slow learning pupils. The point was made by several teachers that all initial courses should contain a section of work on slow learners and, in view of the comments made by those currently teaching slow learning pupils, the research findings suggest that units on the teaching of basic skills, on child development, psychology and curriculum design could usefully be included as units in all initial teacher training courses.

Other issues of concern to teachers were wide in compass and included the balance of time staff spent with slow learners and with other pupils, and the importance of establishing and maintaining liaison with other staff members as well as with parents, feeder schools and outside support agencies. A number of staff felt that slow learner education offered little in the way of a career structure and that promotion opportunities were few; the survey, however, showed that three out of every four teachers in charge of slow learner provision were on scale 3 appointments or above, suggesting that this perception of the status of slow learner education might be in need of some revision. Staff were concerned to see that the curriculum for slow learning pupils was planned as a whole, that the question of optimum group size and structure was considered and that suitable identification procedures were adopted in schools to pinpoint pupils who were slow at learning, and thus to make apropriate provision for their needs. Other issues included the early detection of slow learning pupils in the primary sector, a call for an improvement in the staff/pupil ratio and a concern over those pupils for whom no special provision was made but who required some extra support in order to maintain progress in the mainstream. By far the most frequently mentioned issue was teacher training and the preparation of staff to work with slow learning pupils, as one in three of the staff felt that too few initial or in-service courses concerned with slow learners were currently available.

Chapter six

Curriculum: Years 1 to 3

If the curriculum is to be differentiated in order to meet the special needs of the slow learners, then at what point (if any) does that very differentiation become a separatist device, in that it 'cuts off' the slow learners from the common aspects of the curriculum which contribute to cultural and social cohesion in our society?
(Brennan, 1979)

6.1 Introduction

Previous chapters have been concerned with the organization of remedial provision, the methods by which slow learners were identified and the staff who were responsible for teaching them. The aim of this chapter is to explore the nature of the curriculum and to document some of the lessons which were provided for slow learning pupils. The first section reviews the subjects offered to slow learners, the timetables followed by slow learners and mainstream pupils and the lessons which were observed. In the second section, two pupils' days are described in order to show the effects of the curricular organization and lesson content on individual slow learners in the classroom. In the third section the policies and practices of schools and the implications of these for pupils with learning difficulties are discussed.

6.2 Curricular Differences

Survey data and information obtained during visits to schools showed that the curriculum provided for slow learners frequently differed from that provided for others in the same year group. One difference was in the range of subjects taught. In 42 per cent of secondary schools, slow learners aged 11+ in their first year were not offered the full range of subjects; in 55 per cent of schools the range of subjects was restricted for slow learners in their second year and in 64 per cent of schools the curriculum was restricted in year three. Details appear in Table 6.1.

Table 6.1: *Range of subjects offered to slow learners in years 1, 2 and 3 in secondary schools*

Year Group	No. of Schools Full Range		Restricted Range		Total
	N	%	*N*	%	
Year 1: 11+	339	(58)	245	(42)	584
Year 2: 12+	283	(45)	350	(55)	633
Year 3: 13+	244	(36)	425	(64)	669

No response – 25 schools.

Modern languages was the subject most frequently omitted from the curriculum. Forty-one per cent of schools did not offer modern languages to slow learners in year 1 (11+); this figure rose to 54 per cent in year 2 and to 61 per cent in year 3. Other subjects commonly excluded from the curriculum included science and the separate humanities of history and geography. Approximately 5 per cent of schools in the survey restricted the curriculum for slow learners by two or more subjects.

The Curriculum in Case Study Schools

Seven of the schools visited did not provide modern languages for slow learners and it was found that in five of these pupils took extra English, in one the time was re-allocated to some additional English and European studies, and in the other French lessons were replaced by extra periods in English, geography and mathematics.

Another major difference concerned the time allocated to different subjects. It was observed that slow learners in many schools spent more time than did mainstream pupils on English literacy skills. The time allocated to each subject per week for slow learners and for other pupils aged 11+ in 14 schools visited is given in Table 6.2. In the ten schools in which slow learners spent more time on English than did mainstream pupils, this ranged from one extra lesson per week to an extreme case where slow learners spent 15 out of 40 lessons per week on English compared with the six provided for mainstream pupils.

In some schools the extra time spent by slow learners on basic skills resulted in time devoted to other subjects being reduced. For example in one school slow learners spent less time than mainstream

Table 6.2: *Allocation of curricular time to slow learners aged 11+ in their first year of secondary education†*

Subject Area	Differences in Time Allocated to Slow Learners as Compared with Mainstream Pupils are Recorded in Minutes									
	Secondary								Middle	
	A	B	D	G	I	J	K	X	L	M
English	+ 35	+315	+210	+420	+140	+135	+40	+35	+70	+175
French	−140	−175	−210	−175	−140	−	−120	−	−70	−175
European Studies	+105	−	−	−	−	−90	−	−	−	−
History	−	−	−	−105	−	−45	−	−	−	−
Geography	−	−	−	−70	−	−45	+40	−	−	−
RE	−	−35	−	−	−	−	−	−	−	−
Drama	−	−	−	−	−	−	−	−35	−	−
Maths	−	−35	−	+140	−	+90	+40	−	−	−
Science	−	−70	−	−210	−	−45	−	−	−	−
Music / Art / Craft Subjects / PE/Games / Other Subjects‡	No differences in curricular time allocations.									

†Four of the secondary schools which allocated the same amount of curricular time to all pupils for every subject are excluded from this table.
‡Other subjects included Welsh, social education and current affairs.

Table 6.3: *Percentage of the curriculum taught by remedial staff to slow learners in year 1 (11+)*

School	Mainstream Organization	Main Provision for Slow Learners	English	European Studies	RE	Geography	History	French	Maths	Science	% of Total School Week
			%	%	%	%	%	%	%	%	%
H	Mixed ability	Withdrawal	5	–	–	–	–	–	–	–	5
L	Mixed ability	Withdrawal	5	–	–	–	–	–	–	–	5
X	Mixed ability	Withdrawal	8	–	–	–	–	–	–	–	8
C	Mixed ability	Withdrawal	13	–	–	–	–	–	–	–	13
F	Mixed ability	Withdrawal	17	–	–	–	–	–	13	–	30
D	Sets		30	–	–	–	–	–	15	–	45
E	Sets		13	–	–	–	–	13	–	–	26
B	Bands	Special classes	38	–	–	–	–	–	12	–	50
I	Bands	Special classes	25	–	–	5	–	–	15	–	45
K	Bands	Special classes	17	–	6	8	–	–	14	–	45
J	Bands	Special classes	23	7	7	7	7	–	20	–	71
G	Bands	Special classes	◀—— Literacy 43 ——▲					–	◀Numeracy 22 ▲		65
A	Streams	Special classes	10	7	5	8	–	–	15	–	45
M	Streams	Special classes	25	–	–	–	–	–	–	–	25

pupils on RE, science, and mathematics. In another, extra English and maths for slow learners resulted in their spending less time than their peers on geography, history, science and European studies.

In all of the case study schools there were many other variations in the curriculum provided for slow learners in addition to those which could be seen from an examination of pupils' timetables. One of these was the extent to which remedial staff were responsible for the lessons provided for the slow learners. In every school visited slow learners were taught by both remedial teachers and subject specialists, but the time spent with remedial staff was found to vary from five to 71 per cent of the school week, depending upon the type of provision available and the numbers of subjects for which remedial staff were responsible, as shown in Table 6.3. As reported previously in Chapter five, in some schools slow learners were taught only English/literacy skills by remedial staff, while in others they were taught English literacy skills and a number of other subjects. Where there were special classes, slow learners were commonly taught academic subjects by remedial staff, and practical subjects, such as art, craft, PE and music, by subject specialists.

6.3 The Syllabus

Discussion with both remedial teachers and subject specialists revealed many differing attitudes towards the type of syllabus which was considered most appropriate for slow learners to follow. In some schools the head of the remedial department had devised a special syllabus for use in slow learner classes or within the remedial band. This might include all subjects or cover only those taught by remedial staff. In some cases the syllabus for slow learners was completely different from that followed by mainstream pupils and in others it was found to be an adaptation of the mainstream syllabus.

In some schools where there was close liaison between the head of the remedial department and subject specialists, the latter taught slow learners from a syllabus devised by the remedial department. However, in certain other schools, where remedial staff took no curricular responsibility for slow learners beyond the subjects which they taught, decisions concerning the use and interpretation of the mainstream syllabus with slow learners were left to the specialist teachers concerned. Some subject teachers who felt that all pupils in the same year group should be given the same experiences therefore used the mainstream syllabus for everyone, but others who considered the mainstream syllabus to be unsuitable for slow learners taught a specially designed alternative.

It was found that on occasion some teachers did not adhere to any written syllabus. For example in one instance slow learners were taught phonics during a lesson which was timetabled for RE because the teacher felt that the pupils needed more time to practise basic skills, and on another occasion a biology specialist spent the lesson playing a spelling game because he felt that the mainstream syllabus was not suitable for slow learners and the remedial department had not provided an alternative scheme.

In all schools, English/literacy skills were taught by remedial teachers, and in 12 of the 14, where this basic skills teaching was designed to provide for the needs of individual pupils, the mainstream syllabus, where all followed the same course, was therefore deemed inappropriate and slow learners followed individual programmes. Such lessons were usually based on the acquisition of language skills with emphasis on the technicalities of language, e.g. phonics, spelling, sentence construction. In the other two schools visited, remedial teachers adapted the mainstream syllabus and lessons were frequently based on stories, plays or on a topic of current interest and language skills work arose out of the pupils' responses to these. Another variation was noted in schools where slow learners spent some English lessons with remedial teachers who concentrated on literacy skills and other lessons with subject specialists who taught English in its wider sense through topics and literature. The latter was considered to provide slow learners with a 'balanced' English/literacy programme.

Mathematics lessons were taught by remedial teachers in some schools and by subject specialists in others. Most of the remedial teachers who taught mathematics used a specially devised syllabus which in some schools was based on computational skills and in others on topics considered to be suitable for slow learners. Such syllabuses were usually compiled by remedial and subject staff together. When maths specialists taught slow learners, there were variations in the syllabus followed according to the type of group in which pupils were taught, viz. special class, slow learner set or mixed ability group. For the special classes or sets, subject specialists usually provided work which was planned specifically for slow learners, while in mixed ability groups the mainstream syllabus was invariably followed by the whole class.

For academic subjects other than English and maths, the opinions of teachers concerning the use of a mainstream or special syllabus and the practices observed in the schools were even more diversified. Where remedial teachers taught humanities or science there was usually a specially devised syllabus. Some of these teachers felt that all lessons should be 'child centred' and that all work should arise from the interests of the pupils. Others, together with some of the subject specialists, felt that lessons should be based on common topics but that the teaching methods and resource materials used with slow learners should be specially designed. Some subject specialists believed that all pupils, including slow learners, should be taught from the same syllabus, using the same resource materials and teaching approaches. For practical subjects and PE, subject specialists generally used the same syllabus for all pupils in a year group.

6.4 Classroom Organization and Teaching Methods

The lessons observed included English, mathematics, humanities, science and practical subjects taught by both remedial staff and subject specialists. There were certain factors however which influenced classroom activities irrespective of subject. The size of the group or class in which a slow learner was taught obviously affected the amount of individual attention which a pupil could or was likely to receive from the teacher during a lesson. Slow learners were taught individually, in groups or in classes, which in case study schools were observed to contain up to 27 pupils. It was only where slow learners were withdrawn for English/literacy skills that the groups were small enough for pupils to receive any sustained individual attention. In all other subjects observed, slow learners were taught either in special classes or sets which ranged in size from nine to 20 pupils or in mixed ability classes which contained 25 or more. In these larger classes individual attention was limited to brief exchanges between pupil and teacher. Further evidence of this appears in Appendices 6A.1 and 6A.2 which show the aggregate amounts of time individual pupils were observed to spend with the teacher in English and maths lessons.

The size of the group also influenced the teaching mode employed. When groups were small the teacher was able to work with each pupil individually for part of the lesson and could always be in close proximity to give help and encouragement when it was needed. In larger groups, there was a greater need for the teacher to exercise formal methods of class control. Instead of working with individuals throughout, the teacher either taught the class as a whole or organized activities for individuals or groups and then adopted a supervisory role. Pupils were frequently required to work alone for the whole or part of a lesson. The division of time between class teaching and individual work in mathematics and English lessons appears in Appendices 6A.1 and 6A.2. Similar patterns were also observed in science and humanities lessons.

The tasks which were required of pupils in different subjects could be categorized into three types: namely, 'one-off' tasks specific to individual pupils, 'ongoing' tasks, and the tasks associated with, or arising from, the class teaching component of a lesson. Individual tasks, tailored to the needs of specific pupils and consisting of small units of work such as spelling, phonics or handwriting were only found in the small literacy withdrawal groups. The 'ongoing' tasks, consisting of exercises through which pupils were required to work for the whole or part of a lesson, were observed most frequently in English or mathematics lessons where pupils were working at their own pace using sets of workcards or textbooks. The units of work based on class teaching could usually be finished within the lesson but were occasionally started in the lesson and finished off for homework. Such tasks took many forms, depending upon the subject. In English, for example, pupils were required to write stories and poems based on the lesson topic, or to complete specific tasks from books, worksheets or the blackboard. In mathematics, practice exercises were set after examples had been worked through by the teacher. In humanities and science, tasks relating to the lesson topic introduced by the teacher were set following a practical demonstration, a film, class discussion or some other form of whole class activity. Observed examples of such tasks included the drawing of weather symbols, conducting of experiments, drawing of maps and diagrams and the answering of questions from worksheets.

Pupils responded well to tasks which were tailored for their individual needs and also to the units of work which followed on from a class lesson topic. In general, they were observed to respond well if the demands were clearly defined and the task was a readily identifiable unit. Observed pupils did not respond well to the 'ongoing' tasks; in many instances when they were required to continue working from workcards or from a textbook they wasted time and spent much of the lesson 'off task'. This could have been because they did not understand the instructions or the text or because the tasks were not complete units, but the fact that pupils were observed to work desultorily at such exercises suggests a lack of motivation rather than of understanding on their part. A task which could not be completed during the lesson gave pupils little chance to reach a specific goal and is likely to have contributed to their lack of application. Typical 'off-task' activities included daydreaming, talking and laughing with others about non-work topics, watching sports and games from windows which overlooked playing fields, idly watching others at work in class and, more unusually, taking laced-up shoes on and off, unpacking and repacking a schoolbag and surreptitiously unwrapping and eating sweets. It was interesting to note that the search for resources frequently signalled a period of 'off-task' activity: some pupils made the most of this opportunity to move about the classroom and did not apply themselves to the task of locating the required materials until reminded by the teacher, while others, who failed to find the desired workcard or book immediately, then turned their interest towards other 'off-task' activities.

The teacher was of course the key to the 'successful' lesson, i.e. the lesson in which pupils were engaged on tasks appropriate to their needs. It was the teacher's responsibility to choose the topics, to plan the activities, to provide the materials, to communicate the purpose of the work to pupils and to present the lesson. If the topic was interesting to the pupils and the lesson carefully structured, incorporating a variety of resources and with tasks that were clearly defined, pupils were observed to respond well. However there were many different types of lesson which contained all of these elements. In classes consisting entirely of slow learners, pupils responded more readily when the lesson was teacher directed throughout, and where several different kinds of activity were involved, than they did when one task was set for the whole lesson. One such example was a science lesson in which slow learning pupils were preparing six different gases to find which would relight a glowing splint. After the teacher's demonstration, pupils worked in groups conducting their own experiments and the teacher regularly called the class together to check on progress and results. Another was a mathematics lesson where a teacher gave examples of fractions and circles and finally the construction of a pie-chart. When slow learners were taught in mixed ability groups it was found that different teaching strategies could be successful. For example, teachers introduced topics through discussion or a visual stimulus and then pupils used worksheets based on the topic to direct their individual contributions and records. Worksheets were the same for all pupils but the tasks increased in difficulty to cater for all abilities. In other lessons pupils were presented with a wide choice of tasks within a given framework. The topic in one case observed was measurement; pupils had been introduced to this in a previous lesson and a selection of worksheets and a variety of resource materials was provided. Pupils were given the opportunity to measure different items and to carry out experiments. Three teachers were available to help and advise but not to direct pupils' activities. In each case the lessons observed were closely directed by the teacher, materials were prepared beforehand and the demands made of pupils were clearly defined.

Conversely, in lessons which lacked structure or in which resources were insufficient in number or inappropriate in level or where tasks were not clearly defined, pupils were observed to respond less well. For example, many were 'off task' for much of the time for one or more of the reasons given above. One extreme example occurred where a pupil was observed to be 'off task' for a whole lesson. There was no formal introduction to this lesson in which pupils were required to continue working at their own rate from a book which gave practice in basic literacy skills. During the 35 minute lesson this pupil talked to others, fetched rulers from another room, took off his shoe, swung on his chair, called out to the teacher and to other pupils, chewed his pen, took off his other shoe, untied his shoelaces and put his shoes on again, but he did no work. The teacher, meantime, was attempting to hear individual pupils read. In this case an unstimulating lesson, plus a series of low level and repetitive tasks, combined to create a situation in which the pupil was not in the least motivated to apply himself to work.

Remedial provision is part of the educational programme provided for the slow learner and consequently should be viewed in the context of the whole curriculum. The following accounts of two pupils' days have been selected to illustrate how differences in remedial provision can affect pupils' classroom experiences. For each pupil, the account is drawn from field notes taken during one observation day. (Full details of the research methodology appear in Chapter one, Section 1.3.)

Philip

Philip was in his first year at secondary school and was aged 12 at the time of the observation. He attained a score of 7.6 years on the *Spar* reading test and had entered the school the previous September with a reading age of 6.11 years and a recommendation that he receive remedial help. Philip was a member of a special class of 20 pupils who were taught together for all subjects throughout the day. They spent the four morning lessons on literacy skills with a remedial teacher who set three tasks: to make a Christmas card, to complete a workcard and to undertake a section of quiet reading. Pupils could tackle the tasks in any order they chose. For the first 35 minutes, Philip made a Christmas card. Then, he spent ten minutes finding a pencil, choosing a workcard, attempting to read it, replacing it, choosing another and conferring with a friend. Noting this, the teacher asked Philip to read to her. He read to the teacher for two minutes and then continued reading alone for a further five. Next, he attempted one question on a workcard. After break Philip attempted to continue with the workcard in a desultory fashion and was actively 'off task' for another 35 minutes. He put up his hand briefly, but the teacher did not appear to notice, so eventually he corrected his own work from an answer card. This took eight minutes. He then briefly read aloud with a friend and spent the last nine minutes of the lesson leafing through the book, fixing a page into a folder, fiddling with his pen, watching others, finally clearing up and chatting to the teacher about the next lesson.

After lunch the special class spent two lessons with a home economics specialist. For the first ten minutes Philip listened quietly as the teacher called the register and explained the method for making peppermint creams. Ten pupils, including Philip, did practical work and six written work, as bench space for practical work was limited. For 25 minutes, Philip followed the instructions, demanding frequent reassurance and attention from the teacher. Having decided that he wanted one particular pastry cutter which was already in use, he spent the next 20 minutes waiting for it. He wandered about, talking to others and by the time he acquired the cutter the lesson was about to end. The others cleared up and went to the next lesson, for which Philip arrived eight minutes late.

The last double lesson of the day was European studies with the same remedial teacher who had taught the class that morning. The teacher was checking homework, but Philip had forgotten his. The lesson which was focusing on new towns involved ten minutes of class discussion and 20 minutes of written work based on this. Philip paused and looked around frequently during the time allocated for written work but completed what was required of him. For the last 25 minutes of the lesson he joined in play reading with the whole class.

Most of this pupil's day was spent with one remedial teacher who used a syllabus which was specially devised for slow learners. The subject specialist who taught home economics used the same syllabus for all classes in the year group. Philip was observed to be off task for 39 per cent of the first block of lessons during the morning, when it was left to the pupils to decide when to begin a new task and indeed which new task to begin. In the more tightly structured practical home economics lesson, he spent 18 per cent of the time off task, merely because of a wish to use a particular piece of equipment. During the final lesson of the day, in which three specific kinds of activity were organized by the teacher, he applied himself well, spending only eight per cent of the lesson 'off task', in searches for equipment and in pausing during writing tasks to watch others at work. In this pattern it is interesting to note that most time was wasted during what is usually one of the best working periods in any pupil's day, i.e. the morning hours and that the least amount of time was spent off task in a lesson at the end of the day, often a particularly difficult time for both teachers and pupils. From this analysis it appeared that this pupil in a special slow learner class worked best when the teacher set specific tasks, checked their completion and from time to time engaged the group in a corporate activity such as class discussion or play reading.

Carol

Carol spent most of her day in a mixed ability class of 27 pupils and was taught by subject specialists for all but one of the observed lessons. Her reading age was recorded as 8.3 years (Holborn) in the June before entry and her junior school report recommended that she receive remedial help. (Unfortunately no *Spar* reading age results are available since the school declined to participate in the testing programme.) Throughout her first year, Carol was withdrawn for individual help with literacy during four of the six English lessons each week. It was school policy to withdraw pupils whose reading age was below 8.6 for four lessons, those with a reading age of 8.6 to 9.6 for two and pupils whose reading age was between 9.6 and 10 years for one lesson per week. The first two lessons observed were English in the mixed ability class. Exercise books were returned and Carol read the comments about her work. In the meantime class discussion on pets had begun, led by the teacher, who encouraged everyone to participate. She read short items to stimulate and guide the discussion and also to illustrate different types of writing. After a few minutes, Carol began to show interest in the discussion, only answering one direct question but following the extracts as they were read. At the end of a 40 minute discussion, pupils were asked to write a description or a story about a pet or alternatively instructions on how to look after an animal. Carol settled down at once and wrote for 25 minutes until the end of the lesson. She spent a total of only five minutes off task during the 65 minute lesson.

The following lesson was mathematics, taught by a subject specialist. The aim of the lesson was to give pupils practical experience in measuring angles, which would help them to grasp the basic concepts of this topic. They were working at their own rate through a series of booklets in which the tasks were graded in difficulty. After the first five minutes Carol asked the teacher for help, and again after a further ten minutes; but after the second short explanation she worked largely on her own for 20 minutes, only occasionally stopping to ask other pupils about the work. Throughout the lesson she attempted to complete the specified tasks and did not waste more than five minutes in pausing to chat to others or to look round the room.

The next lesson was spent in the coaching department, where Carol was given individual tuition by one of the remedial team. She responded well, spending approximately half of the lesson reading to the teacher, a third of the time on writing, spelling and sentence construction and the remainder of the time discussing the work.

In the afternoon Carol rejoined her class for needlework. First, she listened to the teacher holding a discussion about sewing equipment. Each pupil was then given an information sheet which the teacher read through before demonstrating the use of different controls on a sewing machine. Carol listened and watched carefully and when the pupils were told to ¡practise setting the controls and stitching straight lines on paper she worked with two other girls. Together they discussed the task, asked the teacher for some advice and used the machine successfully, until the end of the lesson. Carol was interested and involved throughout, spending only two minutes off task.

The last double lesson of the day was art. The teacher spent the first 20 minutes returning pictures to pupils, commenting and giving advice on how best work might continue. After this instruction Carol fetched wool, scissors and glue for herself and a friend and quickly settled down to work cutting and sticking for the next 40 minutes. Without being asked she then collected glue pots and spatulas which she washed up and put away, as the lesson was drawing to a close. For the last five minutes the teacher discussed colour combinations; Carol sat still and listened but did not join in. Again, although pupils were left to work on their own, the stimulus at the start of this lesson, combined with a clear directive about the task to be completed, resulted in a high rate of participation among all pupils throughout.

Conclusions Drawn from Observation in Two Schools

These accounts of two pupils' days illustrate how very different can be the educational experiences of a first year slow learning pupil in a comprehensive school. These two examples were selected because they provided contrasts in the nature of the slow learner provision, in the organization of the curriculum and in the teaching strategies adopted. Remedial staff often have more opportunity to tailor work specifically to the group within their care, and in this situation are less pressured about the 'speed' of progress than are many subject teachers. Yet in a class of 20 pupils this may still present organizational and pedagogical problems as some may be ready to move on to new sections of work while others are still struggling to master the task in hand. Remedial staff have an enviable opportunity to choose how best to use the time at their disposal to meet the needs of individuals within a group of slow learning pupils.

Both pupils had an eight period day, of which Philip spent six and Carol one with a remedial teacher. This was representative of the pattern repeated each week (Table 6.3) as Philip in School G spent 65 per cent of the week with remedial staff and followed a special syllabus in contrast with Carol in School X who spent eight per cent of the week with remedial staff on an individual remedial programme but otherwise followed the mainstream syllabus. Thus Carol spent less time on literacy skills than Philip but she was given individual attention during a withdrawal period whereas Philip was taught literacy skills in a class of 20 pupils. The size of the group necessarily reduced the amount of sustained individual attention it was possible to give each pupil, tasks were not tailored to the needs of each child and in this situation Philip was frequently observed to be 'off task' during the literacy skills lessons. Carol however was kept 'on task' because she had the full attention of the teacher throughout. All of Philip's English lessons were taught by remedial staff, but Carol spent some with a remedial teacher and others with a subject specialist. In this and other mainstream subjects, teaching strategies and materials were designed to ensure that she could participate fully in lessons at her own level. During these lessons she followed the mainstream syllabus, was offered similar learning experiences to her peers and had the opportunity to meet a number of subject teachers. Philip, in contrast, spent only two lessons out of eight with a subject teacher, who used the mainstream syllabus. He did not have an opportunity to mix with other pupils in the year group because the special class was taught as a unit for all subjects. Contact with subject specialists was restricted to the practical areas of the curriculum as it was school policy for slow learners to be taught basic skills and the major 'academic' subjects by remedial staff.

6.5 Discussion

Many devices were used in sample schools in order to provide for the curricular needs of slow learners. In many cases French was replaced by English (Table 6.1), slow learners spent more time than did other pupils on basic skills (Table 6.2) and remedial teachers were responsible for one or more subjects (Table 6.3). Attempts were made to provide for individual needs in English/literacy skills lessons (Appendix 6A.1), and in maths lessons slow learners were given the opportunity to work at their own pace (Appendix 6A.2). In other subjects, special courses were designed or the mainstream syllabus adapted and a variety of different methods and materials were used in the classroom to cater for a variety of individual needs.

Wide variations in school policy towards slow learners resulted in a range of different curricular practices. At one end of the spectrum was the policy of providing slow learners with an educational programme substantially different from that of their mainstream contemporaries. An example of this was provided by Philip's school, where slow learners spent 65 per cent of the school week with remedial staff who taught all the academic subjects from a special syllabus which was followed by all slow learners in the remedial band. This syllabus comprised a detailed literacy scheme which incorporated humanities subjects and a numeracy scheme which also included general science. Remedial staff selected appropriate methods and materials but worked within a framework in which all tasks 'circled out from the child and back to the child', i.e. were designed to extend the frontiers of the child's knowledge while at the same time relating what was learned back to some part of his own experience. Another variation implemented by many schools was a policy that slow learners should be taught 'academic' subjects by remedial staff who had a specialist understanding of pupils' learning difficulties. It was considered that teaching strategies should differ but that the syllabus should be an adaptation of the one followed by the mainstream, so that all pupils of the same age received similar kinds of learning experiences. In one of the case study schools which provided such an example, slow learners spent 71 per cent of the school week with remedial staff, who taught an adapted mainstream syllabus for all academic subjects except science. This was taught by a science specialist with a remedial teacher giving in-class support to slow learners during the lesson.

Another variation in policy was that slow learners should have a different syllabus for the basic skills of literacy and numeracy only, and that for other academic subjects they should follow the mainstream syllabus or a modified version of it so that pupils all learned about the same topics. Again, it was found that different methods and materials were often used to accommodate the special needs of pupils in the slow learner sets, which were the most usual mechanism for implementing this policy. This system was adopted in one school in which the remedial staff were responsible for all English and maths while humanities and science subject specialists liaised with the head of the remedial department in order to ensure that the materials and methods which they used in the mainstream were appropriate for the needs of slow learning pupils.

At the other end of the spectrum there was the policy of providing slow learners with all the same opportunities as their peers and making remedial provision by withdrawing them for individual or small group tuition in literacy skills. In this case, slow learners were taught alongside their mainstream contemporaries, frequently in mixed ability classes in which consideration was given to a wide range of individual needs and ideally, activities and tasks were planned so that pupils could respond at their own level. Carol's school exemplified this, with the rationale that 'Coaching all of the time does no good. Even with extra help, for some pupils, progress will always be slow in reading and writing but this does not mean that they will not get enjoyment or understanding from other lessons which are not so dependent on reading or writing skills.' All subject teachers in this school were aware that each class contained a wide range of ability and lessons were planned so that all pupils could participate fully. Close liaison between subject teachers was maintained, to ensure that all classes were taught from the same syllabus and all pupils in a year group had similar educational experiences and opportunities.

Although almost every school made some form of provision for pupils with learning difficulties, it appeared that in some cases this had been planned without reference to the other curricular components or to the nature of the resulting educational programme. In some schools, for example, the responsibility of remedial staff extended only as far as the subjects they taught, hence subject specialists, who were often uncertain as to the needs of slow learners in mainstream groups, received no help or guidance. Some systems of remedial provision implemented had distinct disadvantages for slow learners. A different syllabus, for example, made transfer to another class or group difficult if not impossible to arrange. Extra English lessons could mean that a slow learner spent less curricular time on other subjects. Special classes were smaller than mainstream ones in order that slow learners could receive individual attention for their specific needs, but observation showed that it was still very difficult in these groups for teachers to provide sustained individual attention or to meet the needs of pupils with a wide range of learning difficulties. 'Individual tasks' often consisted of workcards or textbooks through which pupils worked at their own pace, frequently with much time wasting. Some of the special lessons were limited in content and the level of teacher expectation was not high.

Differences in the balance of the curriculum followed by mainstream and by slow learning pupils were recorded by many schools (Table 6.1). Commonly, slow learning pupils in the lower secondary years followed a restricted curriculum in which certain subjects were not available to them. As Table 6.2 ilustrates, the most usual practice was to remove foreign language time and to increase English language teaching by the same amount. Another strategy frequently implemented was a reduction in the time slow learners spent on certain other areas of the curriculum and a corresponding increase in the amount of time spent on basic skills. In such situations the resulting curriculum for slow learning pupils displayed considerable differences in content and in balance from that followed by mainstream pupils. For example, where English coaching was confined to the teaching of basic skills, slow learners could miss other equally important aspects of literature and the use of language. Similarly, in maths, lessons for slow learners commonly focused on computational skills, as it was felt that they could not cope with topic work until the basic skills had been mastered. However, a wider application of such skills could have been beneficial. In other 'academic' subjects, observations of special classes led us to the conclusion that some lessons for slow learners were unnecessarily limited in content and in depth and failed to extend the pupil fully. Lengthy periods of repetitive exercises proved unstimulating for many slow learners and were observed to lead to inattention and time wasting among younger pupils.

In this context, comments contained in the Bullock Report (1975), which was primarily concerned with reading and language diffi-culties, can well be applied to aspects of the curriculum provided for slow learners. 'There is no mystique about remedial education, nor are its methods intrinsically different from those employed by successful teachers anywhere. The essence of remedial work is that the teacher is able to give additional time and resources to adapting the methods to the individual child's needs and difficulties.' A fundamental question raised by this research on slow learners is how best to structure a pupil's learning programme so that a balance is achieved in terms of curricular content, resource variety, teacher guidance, opportunity for independent learning and group discussion which is appropriate for the pupil at his particular stage of development. The curricula explored in this chapter serve to illustrate how some schools have approached the challenge for slow learners in one year group.

Chapter seven

Curriculum: Years 4 and 5

7.1 Introduction

In this chapter the core subjects provided for all pupils after the third year are documented, options available for less academically able students are investigated and a study is made of the special courses provided for slow learning pupils, including link courses, work experience and community service as well as the public examinations for which they were prepared. Case studies are used to illustrate some of the programmes provided, and the factors which influenced their design are explored.

7.2 Core Subjects and Options

Over 95 per cent of schools in the sample reported that a common core of subjects was offered to all pupils including slow learners in the 4th and 5th years.

The core subjects most frequently mentioned are shown in Table 7.1. All pupils were taught English and maths, while PE and RE were compulsory in most of these schools and offered as options in the rest. In addition to these four subjects, humanities was reported to be part of the core in 30 per cent of schools offering a core curriculum and science in 25 per cent. Only 14 per cent included both humanities and science in the core curriculum at 4th and 5th year level. Other subjects less frequently included in the common core were careers, crafts, home economics, needlework, woodwork, metalwork, French, Welsh, civics, current affairs, health education and music. In all but a few schools the curriculum for pupils in years 4 and 5 comprised a core of subjects plus several options.

Table 7.1: *Core subjects offered to all pupils including slow learners in years 4 and 5†*

Total number of schools with core of subjects for all pupils = 650/671.

Subject	Number of Schools	Percentage
English	650	100
Maths	650	100
PE	631	97
RE	614	94
Humanities	193	30
Science	161	25
Careers	118	18
Art and Design	78	12
Design for Living	71	11

†27 schools, other than middle schools, had no comprehensive 4th year intake and are excluded from this table.

In 42 per cent of the 671 schools in the survey with 4th and 5th year pupils, slow learners were offered a full range of options; in 51 per cent of schools the range of options for slow learners was restricted and in the remaining 7 per cent of schools slow learners were offered a special basic course and no options were available. One such course was described as 'a specially designed total curriculum aimed specifically towards meeting their needs and providing a strong unified motivational force for their final years at school'.

Staff in many of the schools in which a full range of options was offered to slow learners pointed out that this was not always possible to arrange in practice. For example if a modern language had not been studied during the first three years at secondary school, slow learners could not opt to take up this subject in the upper school. Moreover, while options might be open to all pupils, restrictions could arise for slow learners over the level at which a subject was offered. Pupils were counselled in such cases and encouraged to opt for courses 'included specifically for their benefit'.

Where option choices were restricted, a number of methods were employed to accomplish this. In some schools, slow learners were offered all subjects but chose one option less than other pupils. This option was replaced by additional maths or English, compensatory education, basic studies or a 'support' option. In other schools, the less able, or pupils in the lower bands, were offered a restricted list of subjects which were generally less 'academic' than those offered to other pupils. Another form of control was exercised when pupils were required to choose subjects from a number of different 'pools'. Often there was no alternative in a pool which was appropriate for the slow learner who had followed a restricted curriculum in previous years, and sometimes option choices could only be made from the 'pools' which contained the practical subjects, such as art and craft.

Fourteen schools were visited in which pupils aged 14+ were on the roll. In seven of these schools slow learners were offered a full range of options and in seven, option choices were restricted. However, it would appear that the option choice for slow learners is in practice always somewhat restricted, in level if not in subject. The different methods used within the schools visited resulted in major differences in the curriculum provided for slow learners in the 4th and 5th years.

Two out of every three schools with 4th and 5th year pupils reported that the curriculum included courses which were specially designed for slow learners. Although CSE was not originally intended for the least able students, Mode III courses in many of the subjects had been specially designed by teachers for slow learners. These had either a large coursework component or were based entirely upon continuous assessment. In addition, teachers were found to be offering a wide variety of non-examination courses to slow learners, in every area of the curriculum. For example there were special courses in language skills and social English, drama and the theatre arts. Money management, commercial maths and arithmetic in everyday life were among the special courses provided in numeracy, while in science, in addition to many general courses, there were opportunities for rural science, building science, science for society and the biology of home and garden. Local history, Geography for the Young School Leaver, citizen studies and map reading were examples of the many courses offered within the humanities, especially for slow learners, while office practice, typing and business studies were commonly available among commercial courses.

In art and design, slow learner courses were found in pottery, jewellery, printing, textile design and multi-media craft. Other practical subjects specially provided for slow learners included bakery, home management and food studies in addition to the more usual needlework and cookery. Technical courses included vehicle maintenance, building construction and autophysics as well as woodwork, metalwork and technical drawing. The PE element of the curriculum was firmly focused on adult leisure pursuits, and courses in horseriding, seamanship, sailing, orienteering, camping and dancing were recorded. Many courses had been devised to prepare the slow learner for adult life, for example childcare, design for living, work and leisure, consumer education, health and hygiene and first aid.

Some schools also provided opportunities for slow learners to participate in the Duke of Edinburgh's Award Scheme, City and Guilds Foundation courses, and the Schools' Traffic Education Programme (STEP). Another scheme available in a few schools was the Record of Personal Achievement or its equivalent the Record of Personal Experience, which encouraged pupils to compile personal records of activities, interests, achievements and experiences both inside and outside school. This was seen to provide a new kind of objective for school leavers and a new source of information for employers.

7.3 Public Examinations

Over 90 per cent of the schools (632/671) reported that slow learners sat public examinations. The examinations for which slow learners were most frequently prepared were CSE and RSA examinations as shown below:

Type of Examination	Number of Schools	Percentage
CSE Mode I	518	76
CSE Mode III	518	76
RSA	110	16
CSE Mode II	64	9

A few schools entered slow learners for City and Guilds Examinations, Pitman's typewriting, and examinations set by the Union of Lancashire and Cheshire Institute of Typing and Office Practice. Other certificates included the Childcare Certificate of the National Nursery Examination Board, the Hertfordshire Certificate of Proficiency in Mathematics, South West Credits in French, STEP Moped Course, St. John's Ambulance Brigade Adult Certificate, and the Certificate in Extended Education (CEE). Very occasionally, slow learners were entered for GCE O-level examinations. In most schools, slow learners were entered for a variety of different types of examination, the most usual combinations being CSE Modes I and III, which some teachers saw as providing a tangible goal shared in common with other 4th and 5th year students, a factor which encouraged motivation.

7.4 Other Courses Available for Slow Learners

In 37 per cent of schools with 4th and 5th year students, link courses run by the local technical or FE college were available for 4th and 5th year slow learners. These courses, which were generally of a technical, commercial or vocational nature, included brief 'taster' courses open to all pupils as well as examination courses to which only those deemed capable of coping with the syllabus were admitted.

In 57 per cent of the schools, slow learners undertook work experience. In some schools the head of the remedial department made arrangements for one or two pupils to spend a few days working with a local family business, in others an extensive series of visits made to local firms by 4th year pupils was followed by a full programme of work experience for 5th year pupils. Work experience in some schools was linked with the time allocated for careers, so that the continuity of pupils' progress in academic subjects was not affected by periods of time spent out of school.

In 62 per cent of these schools, slow learning pupils in the 4th and 5th year participated voluntarily in community service. Schemes which included assisting in a playgroup or nursery school, serving lunch to old age pensioners and helping with conservation in the countryside were set up and pupils were encouraged to participate. The extent of community service depended very much upon the enthusiasm of the head and staff. In one school visited there was much emphasis on community service and all pupils were 'encouraged to show a practical concern for other members of the community'.

A leaving certificate or some form of testimonial was issued by 35 per cent of schools in the survey. In approximately half of these schools, this was issued automatically to all pupils, while in some schools a certificate was only given on request; in 24 schools, the certificate/testimonial was for slow learners or non-examination pupils only and in five it was designed specifically for Easter or Whitsun leavers. Over half of these certificates or testimonials gave information about academic achievement and personal qualities and sometimes additional information was included about pupils' special interests or hobbies and their contributions to school or to community service. In 27 schools the certificates gave information about academic achievement alone, and in 53 the certificates focused on personal qualities and contributions to school life.

Although in most schools slow learners were provided with a core curriculum and many had the opportunity to make choices from a full range of subjects, differences in subject level and content resulted in pupils following programmes which were significantly different in both the extent of the opportunities they offered and in the nature of the experiences they provided. The case studies which follow outline the programmes provided for 4th year pupils in four schools, and illustrate the ways in which organization, options, special courses and the school's policy towards examinations affected the opportunities and experiences of individual slow learning pupils.

7.5 Case Study Schools

School A

In this small school of 500 pupils, sited in the inner residential area of a large midlands city, each year was organized into four streams, the lowest of which constituted the special slow learner class. Remedial staff taught English, maths, history and geography to pupils in the special class in each of years 1 to 5. The curriculum was restricted, as slow learners did not take French or separate sciences. At the end of the third year slow learners were not offered a choice of options, as were other pupils, but instead followed a course which included English, maths, science, PE and art plus typing, home economics, needlework and child care for girls and metalwork, woodwork, pottery and technical drawing for boys. Pupils spent approximately half of each week with remedial staff and half with subject teachers.

A special 4th and 5th year course which was designed for slow learners and taught by remedial staff aimed to provide 'the education necessary for the pupil to survive in society'. Five units, each taking one term to complete, were used as a focus for practising literacy and numeracy skills and developing communication and social skills. For example the unit on 'The Home' included the drawing of scale plans and the unit on 'Work' incorporated sections on applying for a job and attending an interview. Slow learners did not usually sit public examinations although a special Mode II maths paper was available for those who might wish to do so. Teachers commented on the poor attendance records of many slow learners at this school, a fact which the head acknowledged to be 'a general trend' among the less academic pupils in this age group.

A central issue highlighted by this example is whether these pupils could have achieved more in their years at school. Most slow learners remained in the remedial department throughout their school life as transfer from the special class was very difficult to arrange. The special classes were isolated from the mainstream, their curriculum was different and for 4th and 5th year slow learners no choice of subjects was available. At the end of five years, pupils from this department received a leaving certificate which gave information about reading, numeracy and craft skills, social competence, school attendance and punctuality.

School E

In the first three years at this small rural school, pupils were provided with a broad general education and all followed the same curriculum. Through a complicated pattern of vertical grouping, mixed ability classes, sets and special groups, efforts were made to ensure that slow learners were not isolated from the mainstream but that, where necessary, methods of presenting the mainstream syllabus were adapted to suit their needs.

In the 3rd year all pupils received the same information concerning the subject choices available in the 4th and 5th years. The compulsory subjects were English, maths, PE and social education. The lowest English set was taught by the head of the remedial department and almost all pupils took a public examination in language and/or literature. In maths, pupils were allocated to sets according to their progress, application and school examination results. All classes worked towards public examinations, in which GCE, CSE Mode I or CSE Mode III (limited grade) were available. The social education programme, followed by all 4th and 5th year pupils, was designed to help young people in their attempts to understand themselves, their attitudes and values and to establish their identity. The topics included Self-awareness, Relationships, Our Environment, Study Skills and The World of Work. In PE, as well as traditional team games, there were opportunities for badminton, trampolining, gynmastics, tennis, table tennis and volley ball. Pupils chose five option subjects from a list in which the head of the remedial department ensured that there was always a choice for slow learners. Most subjects were offered at CSE level, and only four non-examination courses were available: namely extra PE, homecare, vehicle maintenance and the Record of Personal Experience. Link courses with the local college of further education were organized and opportunities for community service provided.

In this department the aim was to remedy basic problems during the first three years, so that by the 4th year only a few pupils had difficulties with reading and writing and almost all were taking CSE courses. The head of the remedial department had arranged with the CSE board to overwrite the answers for pupils with severe writing difficulties, where this was deemed necessary. This raises the question of whether or not CSE is a suitable objective for slow learners. In school E, pupils were given the opportunity to participate in examinations; they were expected to achieve academic success and they were observed to respond well to the challenge. Alternative non-examination courses, however well constructed, do not provide the same kind of tangible goal.

The main difference between the two schools lay in the opportunities made available to the slow learners. In school E, all pupils were given the opportunity to study the full range of subjects in the first three years and the setting system was flexible enough to accommodate late developers. In the 4th year, although there were restrictions in the option system, slow learners were able to make a real choice of subjects, most of which were CSE courses.

School D

In this large suburban school, for the first three years slow learners were taught English, maths, science and social studies in sets and other subjects in mixed ability groups. With the exception of French, which was replaced by extra English, they followed the same curriculum as the mainstream.

For all 4th and 5th year pupils, the core curriculum consisted of English, maths, PE, moral and health education, careers, social studies and science. Courses at different levels were provided in the four main curricular areas of English, maths, social studies and science and some option choices could be made from within these broad subject areas. In the English sets, some slow learners were entered for CSE examinations while others worked at extending their basic skills in English. In maths, some slow learners followed a CSE Mode I course, designed for pupils who had some ability in maths but who did not find the subject particularly easy. In this, half of the marks were awarded for a written examination and half for course work. Other slow learning pupils studied non-examination topics providing experience of mathematical techniques and knowledge necessary for everyday life.

As well as English and maths, pupils were required to choose five other courses to include one science, one humanity and one practical subject. In the humanities, options were available in history, geography and environmental studies. This latter course was felt to be particularly appropriate for those pupils who found it difficult to learn a great deal of factual information. In the sciences, slow learners were guided towards the CSE Mode I general science course which included topics such as photography, astronomy, textile science and cosmetics. This course was designed to be as relevant to everyday life and as practical as possible. The rural studies option was offered as a CSE Mode I. In the craft options, pupils could choose O-level or CSE Mode I courses in homecraft or needlework, woodwork, metalwork and technical drawing; non-examination options were available in homecraft and integrated crafts. A range of two-year CSE Mode III link courses was available to all 4th year pupils, but only three 4th year slow learners out of 28 were participating in the construction course at the time of our visit, and none in the commerce or engineering courses. In the 5th year, nine slow learners were taking commercial, construction or engineering courses. All pupils took part in careers programmes and had the opportunity to participate in work experience and community service, but any pupil failing to keep an appointment or misbehaving was not given a second chance. In the 4th year an extensive series of visits to local firms was arranged by the careers department, which also organized work experience for 5th year pupils. All pupils were encouraged to take part in some form of community service but only a few of the slow learners participated in this.

Two questions arise. The first is whether the option choices could have been made wider for slow learners, as all were channelled into the general courses in humanities, science and craft, resulting in much of the week being spent on practical subjects. Also, although they had an open choice from the option list, in practice slow learners were routed into the same groups. The second question is whether the combination of an unbalanced curriculum plus a group of slow learners who spent most of the week together led to the low motivation and lack of interest observed among these pupils and which gave cause for concern in the craft and careers departments.

School X

This was a large modern comprehensive school in a metropolitan area. First year pupils were allocated to mixed ability groups for all subjects and efforts were made to overcome literacy problems by individual or small group withdrawal. Many pupils were withdrawn in the 1st year, but numbers decreased in the 2nd and 3rd years as problems were remedied. Setting was introduced for some subjects, in the 2nd and 3rd year in science, maths and French. Only in French did slow learning pupils follow a different course from others in the year group. In the 4th and 5th year the core curriculum consisted of English, maths, PE, social studies and a tutorial period. In English, all groups followed a common course which led either to CSE or GCE, and decisions concerning examination entries were not made until the Spring term of the 5th year. In maths, GCE and CSE Mode I pupils followed common topics and only potential Mode III entrants took a separate syllabus from the start of the 4th year. Social studies was a non-examination course for all 4th and 5th year pupils.

All pupils were prepared for public examinations and the slow learners were entered for CSE or RSA, as appropriate, making a choice from 40 of the total of 60 available options. For pupils who were still receiving coaching in the basic skills of reading and writing at the end of the third year, it was recommended that only five choices be made and the sixth option be used for coaching. It was also possible for some pupils to choose the support option, during which slow learners could spend time on any of their other subject choices, with support from a teacher who was sympathetic to their problems. Each year about ten per cent of the year group chose the support option and about half of this number used one other option for additional help with literacy skills. An examination of the timetables of ten 4th year pupils who had all chosen the support option showed that each pupil was studying a different combination of subjects; the most 'popular' being art, physics and rural science, but the selection was wide, including office skills, world religions, music, technical drawing and biology. Work experience had become more difficult to organize, with the national increase in unemployment, but efforts were made to provide placements for some 5th and 6th year pupils who were not following a full programme of examination subjects.

The programme provided for 4th and 5th year slow learners prepared them for CSE examinations and a wide choice of courses allowed them to follow their own interests, ensured a degree of integration and prevented groups of pupils with learning difficulties from being thrown together for a major part of each week. Provision was made for those who were still experiencing learning difficulties by the inclusion of the support option and pupils with severe problems also had the opportunity to receive continued help from the coaching department via the special coaching option.

The philosophy behind the provision made for slow learners in this school was expressed in a comment made by the deputy head.

We are not convinced that there is a clearly identifiable group of slow learning pupils. Standardized tests measure attainment in terms of the items tested. In some cases, differences are influenced by absences, attitude, behaviour, the skills of previous teachers, parental support, etc. There are many variables including changes that take place while pupils grow up and develop their abilities. We attempt to identify and diagnose the needs of pupils who require special help rather than 'organize the education of slow learning pupils'.

7.6 Discussion

These four schools have illustrated some of the wide differences found between the programmes for slow learners in the 4th and 5th years in sample schools. Factors which influenced the structuring of such programmes included the grouping procedures adopted during preceding years and the curriculum followed by slow learners in the lower school. It was found that most pupils in the survey studied a core of subjects plus a selection of options, some of which were specially designed for slow learners and others which were part of the ordinary option system. In some schools, the structure of the option system was such that slow learners had few, if any, real choices to make among the alternatives available; the effects of a restricted curriculum and the fact that certain subjects were only offered to potential GCE candidates combined to produce this situation. In a few schools the staff provided slow learners with a complete specially-designed course, and pupils who had spent all or the greater part of their time being taught by remedial staff in the lower school were routed into this programme.

In schools E and X, 4th and 5th year pupils followed courses in subjects of their choice within an option system which was structured to ensure that a balanced curriculum resulted. In school D, however, although pupils spent time on all curricular areas, the structure of the option system effectively restricted slow learners' choices and channelled them into the same subject groups. In addition, slow learners, who took combined humanities and a general science course, spent less time on each of these subjects than did their contemporaries who took separate sciences, i.e. physics, chemistry and biology or separate humanities, i.e. history or geography. In school A, slow learners were not involved in the option system at all, and were provided instead with a programme of basic skills, some science and art plus a number of other practical subjects.

These four schools represented extreme examples and many

variations on similar themes were encountered in other schools visited. A major issue which emerged was whether slow learners should join classes preparing for public examinations or whether non-examination courses were more appropriate for them. In some schools, such as E and X, almost all courses led to CSE; in others, slow learners could take both CSE and non-examination courses. However, in one such school, where slow learners were taught in special classes from the first to the fifth year, the only CSE examination entries were in art, which five of the 33 pupils were taking. Attendance was found to be generally poor; for example, seven 5th year pupils in one of the special classes had each been absent for more than 50 half-days in the previous term, a trend widely recognized as a regional problem and recorded in the local paper at the time of the visit. To what extent did the kind of programme provided at the school influence the attendance rates of its 4th and 5th year slow learners?

Clearly, a large school has greater resources in terms of staff expertise and could provide a wider range of options than a smaller school, but size was not the sole criterion. For example, school A with 500 pupils and 36 staff offered fewer choices to slow learners than did school E with a roll of 660 and a staff of 35, but it was school policy which exerted the greatest influence on the programmes provided for slow learners in the 4th and 5th years. As these pupils were not tested, it was not possible to quantify the number with learning difficulties nor to comment on the severity of their problems, but the wide range of systems observed reflected considerable differences in the curricular objectives implemented for slow learning pupils in their 4th and 5th years at school. Other factors which affected the programmes provided for slow learners were the nature of the school's catchment area, and the extent of the learning difficulties present among pupils in the 4th and 5th years. As these older pupils were not tested it was not possible to quantify the number with learning difficulties or to comment on the severity of their problems, but the wide range of systems observed reflected considerable differences in the curricular objectives implemented by teachers of 4th and 5th year slow learners.

No chapter on 4th and 5th year pupils would be complete without some comment concerning their future because, to quote one head teacher, 'career problems and prospects pose very serious anxieties for slow children and for their parents'. The attempts made within some schools to provide a broadly-based curriculum for these pupils indicate that staff are well aware of the importance of providing a comprehensive educational programme for slow learners in the upper school. Curricula focusing on the development of pupils' social and life skills in addition to the acquisition of basic litercy and numeracy skills were fairly common, as were CSE Mode III courses. However, schemes containing work experience and/or community education opportunities were less frequently encountered and link courses with local FE colleges even less so.

There is a need for both school and local authority based initiatives to link schools more closely with FE colleges, with industry and with the local community. Schemes such as the ILEA/EEC Transition from School to Work Project, in which ten secondary schools collaborated with five FE colleges to develop a curriculum for underachieving students during their final year of statutory education, might provide a model for other LEAs to consider. Known as 'The Bridging Course' this venture aimed to encourage 'under-achieving young people to take a more responsible look at themselves, their educational prospects and their future'. (From a paper prepared for the 'ILEA Bridging Course' conference, 1 December 1981, Country Hall, ILEA.) School and college staff in each consortium devised, taught and monitored a programme which took students into college for two days a week and into schools for three, to follow a programme covering three main areas; general education, vocational options, and careers education and counselling. Evaluation so far has revealed an encouraging reponse from students and a high incidence of placements in first jobs or FE courses among participating students, while staff have been reviewing methods of assessment and record keeping. The Cooper report (1981), com-missioned by the DES to study links between school and industry, recommended that Chief Education Officers 'should be recognized as the focal points for local advice to schools and industries and for the promotion of initiatives within the area of their local authorities'. With regard to the training of teachers, the recent HMI discussion paper 'Teacher Training and Preparation for Working Life' (DES, 1982) acknowledged that there is 'increasing pressure on schools to assess the relevance of their curriculum to their pupils' future working lives', and indicated interest in developing aspects of initial training courses which would help teachers to prepare pupils for adult life.

Now is the time for a review of the existing educational programmes provided for pupils in their final years at school who are not following traditional academic courses, for an evaluation of present facilities and for the development of new, collaborative initiatives to take place.

Chapter eight

Which Way Now?

8.1 The Organization of Slow Learner Provision

The major issues whose substance constitutes the separate chapters of this report are explored here with a view to identifying pointers for future provision for slow learners in the secondary sector.

Following the introduction, in which an outline of the research methodology was given, Chapter two reported on the many different ways in which headteachers and their staff chose to group slow learners in order to provide the most appropriate learning programmes for their needs. It was common for heads to organize more than one kind of special teaching group for slow learners, in an attempt to cater for different levels of learning difficulty and in certain cases, subject-specific problems. Some pupils were taught in these special groups for the whole of their curriculum while others received remedial tuition in one or two curricular areas only. Provision for slow learners was available from entry to the fifth or even sixth year in some schools while in others it was restricted to a particular year or series of year groups. Details of the advantages and disadvantages associated with specific forms of organization are explored fully in Chapter two; here it is pertinent to record the wider issues which emerged from the investigation.

Three major strands were identified. First, it is apparent that the kind of special provision made for slow learners need not be governed by the organization of the whole school. For example, if it were policy to segregate slow pupils this could be arranged within a banded, setted or mixed ability structure. Separating slow learners from their peers for all or part of the curriculum could be achieved by a series of subject sets as readily as by a special class, and schools adopted both strategies in order to achieve a greater or lesser degree of separation for teaching purposes. However it should also be remembered that the kind of pupil group into which new entrants are placed and taught has a profound effect not only upon their learning but also upon the development of friendships, and can effect the ease and speed with which they adjust to their new surroundings.

A second strand concerned the effect of the special provision on the pupil's total educational programme. For example difficulties could be created by withdrawing a pupil from one or two mainstream lessons causing him to miss work, as well as by teaching an alternative course, thereby limiting future choices. These are but two of a series of related issues centred on the question of how best to provide the most appropriate kind of educational support for slow learners without restricting their curricular opportunities or progress. The third strand is liaison, the importance of which cannot be overemphasized. If a pupil is taught separately from others in the year group, be it in a special class, set or even individually, it is of immense help to the remedial teacher to know what other pupils in the year are learning, particularly in terms of subject content and skills. Without this kind of knowledge, how can a specialist teacher of slow learners fully assess how a pupil is likely to fare on return to the mainstream? Similarly, if the subject teacher is aware of what back-up a pupil is receiving during periods of remedial assistance then he or she can provide reinforcement and monitor subsequent progress in mainstream lessons. Also, when a subject specialist receives a pupil who has previously been taught in another group, knowledge of the kind of work which that pupil has covered is of help in settling the pupil into the new class, or indeed in deciding the most appropriate point to suggest that a pupil might join the class.

At present, teachers have little opportunity to discuss programmes of work in this detailed fashion. Occasionally case conferences can provide a meeting ground, but the pupils have by then often become 'problems'. Our research leads us to the conclusion that increased opportunities for discussion on aims, content, materials and methods between remedial and subject specialists who teach a given year group would be of immense value. Such discussions, preferably timetabled, would provide a much needed meeting ground for all who teach those with learning difficulties.

8.2 Transfer Procedures and the Identification of Slow Learners

In Chapter three the means by which staff identified slow learning pupils among new entrants were explored, details of the information received from feeder schools presented and an account of subsequent testing procedures given. The messages from this section were clear. The research indicated that transfer procedures were generally complex and time consuming; secondary school teachers struggled to draw valid and useful conclusions from a mass of often incompatible information received from typically ten but often up to thirty different feeder schools. Attempts to assess the implications of reading age scores derived from different tests taken at different stages of a pupil's school career and to reconcile the results of a variety of school-based tests and exams and general assessments all took time, and, while class teachers' comments were found to be particularly helpful, staff in many secondary schools preferred to visit the feeders in order to discuss 'borderline', 'slow' or 'problem' pupils about whose placement there was some degree of uncertainty or concern.

Furthermore, in approximately half of the schools in the survey all pupils were tested again shortly after entry, in order to ascertain whether they were suitably placed in teaching groups. In many cases slow learners were then given additional tests, primarily language based. These findings lead us to suggest that a secondary school and its major feeders might with profit work together to design a common transfer document or, more importantly, to decide which tests should be taken by all pupils prior to secondary school entry. Already some local authorities have done this, specifying a series of tests for use throughout the LEA, thus freeing the secondary school from the need to screen all new entrants and providing a database for placements.

The lack of involvement of remedial staff in initial allocation procedures gave cause for concern. In only one secondary school in four were teachers in charge of slow learners involved in arrangements for the placement of new entrants into teaching groups. We believe that remedial staff should be an integral part of the team who receive new entrants into the secondary sector and that their knowledge of the feeder schools and consequent expertise in the interpretation of grades and teacher comments concerning *all* pupils with special learning needs is at present not being fully utilized. We consider that the teacher in charge of remedial education has a key role to play in establishing and maintaining liaison with feeder schools, that he or she should be the chief contact point for all pupils with learning difficulties and be closely involved with testing procedures in the year before transfer. In this way appropriate provision could be made for all pupils with learning problems immediately upon entry to the secondary school.

A further issue which emerged as the transition arrangements were explored more fully concerned the use of test results. The chief criteria used to group all pupils for teaching purposes were class teachers' comments on attainment and attitude to school together with reading age scores. One-third of the schools re-tested all new entrants to establish a reading age score shortly after admission. Acknowledging the central place of literacy skills in the curriculum, teachers were anxious to establish a pupil's reading age relative to chronological age and many also wished to record comprehension levels and facility in spelling. Commonly, the results of non verbal reasoning and reading tests were used to identify pupils whose scores on each differed widely and who were then selected for further testing and diagnosis. Relatively few staff, however, investigated other aspects of a pupil's development such as perceptual and motor coordination skills for example; most 'identification' procedures relied heavily on the results of intelligence and attainment testing. This highlights further the importance of using appropriate instruments.

Teachers are experiencing difficulty in finding a reading test designed for use with pupils aged 11+, which is up to date in vocabulary and norms, discriminates at the lower ability levels and which fits readily into a normal lesson period. The 1978 London Reading Test was found by the team to meet many of these criteria, and in its design the authors state that 'we have borne in mind the needs of teachers who have to screen children for remedial teaching. This means that the test's powers of discrimination are concentrated at the bottom end of the score distribution'. Further, designed for administration to ILEA's multiracial population, the test contains items which do not handicap pupils from any one cultural background. However the test is untimed, with a recommended length of one hour. In addition, it contains an essential practice test which is necessary as many pupils are unfamiliar with cloze procedure. In most secondary schools, therefore, considerable disruption to the timetable would take place if the test were to be administered to an entire year group as a routine screening procedure, a factor which staff would wish to weigh against its undoubted advantages.

There is a need for publishers to review, update and re-design many of the existing tests of reading and language skills. Tests prepared in the 1950s are now dated in terms of vocabulary, presentation and, in many cases, norms. The research study indicated that some schools were attempting to structure their own 'battery' of tests, often by using several commercially produced tests from different sources. The compilation of a test battery is a lengthy and skilled process, necessitating the use of skills additional to those required in interpretation, and involving more time and expertise than is generally available among the staff at a single school. Publishers would do well to consider designing batteries of tests which could be used in secondary schools not only to 'identify' slow learning pupils along a number of dimensions but also to monitor their subsequent progress, particularly in basic skills.

8.3 The Role of Staff who Teach Slow Learning Pupils

In Chapter four, the role of the teacher in charge of slow learners was explored in the context of the major areas of responsibility outlined by the National Association for Remedial Education (NARE). Detailed studies in seventeen schools revealed that although all heads of department were responsible for diagnosing the kinds of difficulties experienced by slow pupils and prescribing appropriate learning programmes, purchasing resources and teaching the pupils, only half of them were involved with the allocation of slow learners to teaching groups: albeit a higher proportion than the whole sample but still far short of what is desirable. The involvement of a staff member who is familiar with many of the test results which come through from feeder schools and who has additional information about the specific learning difficulties of individual pupils is surely advantageous to any team engaged in grouping new entrants for teaching purposes.

It was disappointing to find little evidence of remedial support in mainstream classes; less than three per cent of schools in the whole sample adopted this strategy. Where remedial teachers worked in ordinary classes alongside subject staff they were 'floating', to give help to any pupil who needed it as well as assisting and advising in the production of resource materials. While much has been written about the growth of this aspect of the remedial teacher's role, the research found very little evidence of its existence. Part of the reason can be attributed to the tighter allocations resulting from the falling rolls of the 1980s and subsequent adjustments in the teaching establishment, but there is another aspect. Traditionally, secondary teachers have worked alone with a class or group of pupils. The introduction of another adult into the learning environment is a facet of teaching which many staff find hard to accept and to which some fail to adjust. The schemes which were explored fully illustrated that much depended on the efforts of individual members of staff and that these 'successful' schemes relied heavily upon the personalities of the teachers involved for their survival. They 'worked' because the staff involved co-operated closely, each with a clear role definition and expectation one of the other.

To many, a teacher of slow learners is one who provides remedial assistance for pupils outside the mainstream class. We would argue that there are times when considerable benefit can accrue from the presence of a remedial support teacher in the mainstream class, with the purview of assisting any pupil who obviously requires help but with the primary task of reinforcing the learning of the slow pupils. This kind of co-operation between two adults in a secondary school classroom does not come easily to those used to the traditions of one teacher one class, but the undoubted benefits to all pupils make this a particularly valuable strategy to consider adopting where staffing levels permit. Sympathy with and understanding of the aims of the class teacher are essential on the part of the remedial teacher, whose role is a secondary and supportive one, offering assistance within the framework established and maintained by the subject specialist.

This highlights a wider problem, common in secondary schools, of teachers who work in isolation, knowing little of the other subject areas studied by the pupils whom they teach. The case study research indicated that one way of helping remedial staff to extend their teaching role was to give the teacher in charge of slow learners a title such as 'learning adviser' or a similar name. An adviser could be expected to work outside the traditional remedial area and to advise and consult with others in a way in which a head of department would not. Some staff felt that by consulting a remedial teacher they were in some way admitting their own failure, but the wider role sought by many of those in charge of slow learner provision was found to be facilitated by the adoption of a 'non-traditional' title which crossed departmental and faculty boundaries and was concerned with pupils and their learning difficulties rather than with subject matter.

The scale of the post to which the teacher in charge of slow learner provision was appointed was also found to be important. The research indicated that staff on scale 4 and above were involved with the making of policy decisions and they reported few problems in subsequently implementing these. Staff on scales 2 and 3 however were not automatically involved in such meetings; their position in the school was less powerful and it was not always so easy for them to get new schemes 'off the ground'. In every case, however, the support and involvement of the head was a key factor in ensuring the success of new initiatives in remedial education.

Case studies revealed that the expectations of subject staff were different in schools where there were special classes from those in which withdrawal was the traditional method of providing for slow learners. Where special classes were the norm, little or no liaison between subject and remedial specialists was expected, while, in contrast, informal consultation was likely to take place in schools where slow learners were withdrawn for periods of support work.

The role which a remedial teacher in charge of slow learner provision could be expected to fulfil was thus found to be influenced by a number of factors, which included the name and status of the departmental team and its head, the personality of this teacher, the kind of organizational framework established for slow learning pupils and the consequent expectations of subject specialists. Co-operation and liaison between staff was found to be facilitated in those schools in which a wider role was indicated in the title given to the teacher in charge of slow learner provision.

8.4 Teacher Training

Investigation into the preparation and training of those who taught slow learners, which constituted Chapter five, revealed that the majority had moved into remedial education from other curricular areas. Indeed, four out of every five remedial staff considered that it was very important to gain general teaching experience before specializing in teaching slow learners. Fifty-three per cent of the sample had attended in-service courses concerned with slow learners during the preceding five years and of these two-thirds were heads of department or teachers in charge of slow learner provision. Of all those who attended in-service courses on remedial education, approximately one teacher in five gained additional qualifications by this means. Thus the availability of in-service courses as an information source is of considerable importance to many who teach slow learners and to some affords a valuable means of qualification.

The results of a survey undertaken during the early months of the project in 1979 revealed that for those seeking to join an initial or in-service course on slow learners the search for an appropriate course could be long and difficult. The DES and NATFHE handbooks were far from clear in their methods of presentation and of recording course detail, and it was not always apparent just how great a part the 'slow learner' component played in the course as a whole. For many of the longer courses, secondment was necessary and some intending participants who failed to gain such financial support were unable to take up places offered to them, leaving certain courses which were initially oversubscribed to open with places still unfilled. Although about half of those who had trained since the mid-1970s reported that they had received some training in teaching slow learners, only one-third of those who trained in the early 1970s had done so and far fewer of those who qualified as teachers in previous years had any such specialist training. The survey of training courses available in 1979 found few substantial courses on teaching slow learners available at initial certificate, degree or PGCE level.

Most of the initial and in-service courses in the DES and NATFHE handbooks were located in the larger urban centres, again restricting the choice available to staff who lived outside these areas. The LEA courses, and those run by universities, polytechnics, colleges of education, teachers' centres and professional associations, were more widely spread geographically and although many were non-certificated they provided valuable in-service opportunities for teachers. The importance of these local in-service agencies should not be underestimated. Details from course participants provided insights into the kinds of benefits which they perceived were to be gained from an in-service course on slow learners. Overwhelmingly, the opportunity to meet others who taught slow learners and to discuss their work with them was the single most helpful feature identified by course participants, while the chance to see and use new resources and to gain practical guidance on teaching strategies and in testing were also recorded by at least one participant in ten. Thus teachers were saying that it was not only the course content but the way in which a course was designed that was important; the opportunities which it gave staff to learn from one another, and not only from the course tutor, were perceived as particularly valuable.

Details supplied by tutors of in-service courses listed in the handbooks revealed that over half of these courses focused on testing and the assessment and diagnosis of learning difficulties, on teaching literacy, numeracy and other subjects to slow learners, curriculum design and on issues in special education and psychology. Details from initial training courses revealed a similar pattern, with over half providing units on testing, assessment and diagnosis, on the teaching of literacy skills and on the organization of slow learner provision, and just under half focusing on the identification of slow learning pupils. While some courses were wide-ranging, it appeared that many, at both initial and in-service level, were still narrow in concept and in compass. There is a need to broaden existing initial training courses beyond testing, identification and the teaching of basic skills.

Teachers of slow learning pupils have a new and wider role to play in secondary schools today; preparation for this involves a range of expertise extending beyond the teaching of literacy and numeracy to all areas of the curriculum and involving also the use of liaison and management skills concerned with issues of slow learner education. Course providers would be well advised to review the kinds of demands currently being placed on remedial teachers and to consider these when designing new courses, bearing in mind also the considerable benefits teachers derive from discussion and the opportunity to learn from each other which many courses already provide.

8.5 The Curriculum Followed by Slow Learning Pupils

In Chapters six and seven the curriculum followed by slow learning pupils was explored, in the light of schools' grouping practices and the deployment of subject and remedial staff. Different teaching strategies were observed and pupils' responses to these recorded. In general, slow learners were seen to respond better in lessons where specific tasks were set, using defined resource materials, than in lessons where there was an element of choice. Considerable individual teacher guidance appeared to be necessary where slow learners were required to select materials, to decide which of a series of tasks to undertake first or where they were continuing with an on-going piece of individual work. Observations of 11 year old pupils pointed to the fact that by structuring assignments carefully the teacher could help the slow learner to work towards a series of short-term goals with considerable success. Long-term goals, independent tasks which called for little or no teacher or peer contact, too extensive a range of resource materials and a wide choice of tasks were not observed to assist the slow learning pupil in either motivation or application to work.

The difficulties of providing a properly balanced curriculum for slow pupils in the upper school were highlighted in Chapter seven, where the effects of restricting a pupil's curriculum in the early years of secondary education together with the school's grouping practices and option schemes were found to leave some pupils with little or no choice of upper school courses. Much work remains to be done on the structuring of curricula for less able pupils in the 4th and 5th years; goals need to be established which are acceptable and realistic for both teacher and pupil, couched in terms which parents and future employers can appreciate. Work experience, preparation for adult life schemes and the development of school-based record and profiling systems can go some way towards bridging the present gulf between school and post school experience, whether this be further education, employment or a government-sponsored training scheme. Slow learning pupils require as much support at this level as they do lower down the school: the teaching of basic skills is not enough. If pupils are to be prepared adequately for life in an increasingly competitive outside world they require considerable help and guidance in how to make the best use of the skills they have acquired in school.

8.6 Achieving the Right Balance

The major issues outlined above are all aspects of the central theme of this research: namely, how best to provide for slow learning pupils in secondary schools. The project has shown that while few major changes have taken place during the past decade there is now a growing awareness that the needs of slow learners can be met in a variety of ways, that their education is as much the concern of the subject teachers as of the remedial specialist, that staff can benefit both pupils and themselves by working together in classrooms and by planning courses and designing resource materials co-operatively. There is, however, still a long way to go. In-service training has a big part to play in assisting remedial teachers to adopt a wider role, and subject staff to accept a sharing of responsibility for the education of slowing learning pupils. Initial training, despite cutbacks, should provide input on slow learner education for all students. Psychologists and publishers have a contribution to make in the production of up-to-date test materials; headteachers could ensure that the learning problems of slow pupils are included in school-based inservice programmes, and remedial staff could themselves take the initiative to assist other teachers in the diagnosis of pupils' learning difficulties and in the design of appropriate subject-based provision.

In each of these areas there is an optimum in terms of curriculum design, teaching materials, staff time and pupil grouping which can be said to provide the most appropriate form of special provision for each slow learning pupil. To achieve the right balance is no easy task; it is to be hoped that some of the ideas and advice culled from current practice and contained in this report will assist those involved in planning and implementing provision for slow learning pupils and at the same time offer guidance to those in the process of reviewing such provision in the face of changing circumstances. The report has highlighted factors which are clearly crucial in such deliberations, but the implications for curriculum content, resource production, teaching strategies and the deployment of staff within the organization of each school can only be fully realized by those already working there.

It is the staff of each school who are best placed to assess the nature and extent of the needs of its slow learning pupils and who have the means to set about meeting them in the most appropriate way.

To conclude, as one head teacher explained:

There is no definitive answer to the problems of provision for slow pupils. Questions of practicality are as important as questions of philosophy and the school's resources must be geared for the optimum response to the needs of all pupils. This 'comprehensive' ethos, which considers the individual's differing needs, should ensure that each pupil is valued and respected equally and his needs met to the best of the school's ability.

Appendix 3A.1. *Tests used to identify slow learners among new entrants*

Name of Test	Number of Schools in Which Test Used		
	Secondary (N=698)	Middle (N=93)	Total (N=791)
APU Arithmetic Test	1	–	1
Aston Index	8	–	8
Blackwell Spelling Test	14	–	14
Bristol Achievement Tests: English Language	7	–	7
Bristol Achievement Tests: Mathematics	1	–	1
The Burt Word Reading Test	31	4	35
Carver Word Recognition Test	–	1	1
Cognitive Abilities Test	16	–	16
Culture Fair Intelligence Test	1	–	1
Daniels and Diack Standard Reading Tests: Test 1, The Standard Test of Reading Skill	15	4	19
Daniels and Diack Standard Reading Tests: Test 11, Graded Spelling Test	18	–	18
Daniels and Diack Standard Reading Tests: Test 12, Graded Test of Reading Experience	114	7	121
Daniels and Diack Standard Reading Tests (unspecified)	35	5	40
Diagnostic and Remedial Spelling Manual (Peters)	4	–	4
Dorcan Spelling Analysis	3	–	3
Draw-A-Man Test (Goodenough–Harris Drawing Test)	1	–	1
Edinburgh Reading Tests	7	2	9
English Picture Vocabulary Test	10	3	13
Gap Reading Comprehension Test	32	6	38
Gapadol	20	1	21
Hesse Basic Number Screening Test	3	1	4
Hillingdon Modules (*See* Transitional Assessment Modules)			
Holborn Reading Scale	25	4	29
Jackson Phonic Skills Tests 1-11	9	–	9
The Kingston Test of Silent Reading	1	–	1
The London Reading Test	1	–	1
Moray House Tests (*See* Edinburgh Reading Tests)			

	Secondary	Middle	Total
The Neale Analysis of Reading Ability	33	3	36
NFER			
Verbal Test CD	1	1	2
Verbal Test D	4	–	4
Verbal Test EF	8	–	8
Verbal Test GH	1	–	1
Non-Verbal BD	–	4	4
Non-Verbal DH	46	1	47
Reading Test AD	5	5	10
Reading Test BD	2	2	4
Reading Test EH 1-2	4	–	4
Reading Tests SR-A and SR-B	3	–	3
Reading Comprehension Test DE	4	–	4
Welsh Sentence Reading Test	1	–	1
English Progress Test C2	–	2	2
English Progress Test D2	5	–	5
Basic Mathematics Tests A and B	2	–	2
Basic Mathematics Test DE	4	–	4
Mathematics Attainment Test B	–	2	2
Mathematics Attaintment Test C1	2	1	3
AH2 Group Test of General Ability	7	–	7
AH3 Group Test of General Ability	3	–	3
AH4 Group Test of General Intelligence	4	–	4
Oliver and Boyd Maths Test 1–20	2	–	2
Otis-Lennon Mental Ability Tests	2	–	2
Profile of Mathematical Skills (France)	3	–	3
Raven's Standard Progressive Matrices	18	2	20
Richmond Tests of Basic Skills Levels 1–6	13	2	15
Salford Sentence Reading Test	7	3	10
Schonell Tests			
R1 Graded Word Reading Test	31	7	38
R3 Silent Reading Test A } R4 Silent Reading Test B }	37	1	38
Graded Word Spelling Test S1 or S2	21	–	21
Diagnostic English Test 5: Composition	1	–	1
Essential Mechanical Arithmetic Test	1	–	1
Essential Intelligence Test	2	–	2
Southgate Group Reading Tests	4	1	5
Spar Reading Test (Young)	15	3	18
Spar Spelling Test (Young)	2	2	4
Spooncer Group Reading Assessment	4	2	6

Name of Test	Secondary	Middle	Total
Swansea Test of Phonic Skills	2	–	2
Transitional Assessment Modules	1	–	1
Vernon Graded Arithmetic –			
Mathematics Test (Metric Edition)	9	1	10
Vernon Graded Word Reading Test	1	–	1
Wechsler Intelligence Scale for Children			
(WISC) – Revised	1	–	1
Widespan Reading Test	18	3	21
Yardsticks . . . Criterion-Referenced			
Tests in Mathematics	1	–	1
Young Non-Readers Intelligence Test	5	1	6
Young Group Mathematics Test	4	–	4
Young Group Reading Test	16	3	19

Note:
Other tests used to identify slow learners
for which references could not be given
since insufficient detail was recorded.

	Secondary	Middle	Total
Tests of language skills (reading, phonics)	6	1	7
Tests of number skills (maths, arithmetic)	23	1	24
Unspecified tests (majority 'NFER' or	39	5	44
'Schonell')	—	–	—
	68	7	75

Appendix 3A.2. *Tests used with slow learners in order to gain a profile of their individual capabilities. (It was common for several tests to be used as a battery.)*

Name of Test	Schools Using Test		
	Secondary	Middle	Total
Aston Index	57	8	65
Basic Number Screening Test	2	–	2
Blackwell Spelling Test	11	1	12
Bristol Achievement Tests: English Language	2	–	2
Bristol Social Adjustment Guides	1	–	1
Burt–Vernon Graded Word Reading Test	18	1	19
Burt Re-Arranged Word Reading Test	1	–	1
Cassell Linked English Tests: Attainment Test	1	–	1
Cognitive Abilities Test	1	–	1
Cornwell Orally Presented Group Test of Intelligence for Juniors	1	–	1
Cotterell Check List of Basic Sounds	2	–	2
Crichton Vocabulary Scale	2	–	2
Daniels and Diack Standard Reading Tests (unspecified)	121	13	134
Diagnostic and Remedial Spelling Manual (Peters)	5	–	5
Domain Phonic Tests	14	2	16
Dorcan Spelling Analysis	4	1	4
Draw-A-Man Test (Goodenough–Harris Drawing Test)	4	–	4
Edinburgh Reading Tests	6	1	7
English Picture Vocabulary Test	16	3	19
Eysenck Personality Inventory	1	–	1
Frostig Developmental Test of Visual Perception	5	–	5
Gap Reading Comprehension Test	8	1	9
Gapadol	13	–	13
Gates–MacGinitie Reading Tests	1	–	1
Gates–McKillop Reading Diagnostic Tests	1	–	1
Harris Tests of Lateral Dominance	1	–	1
Holborn Reading Test	17	1	18
Jackson Phonic Skills: Tests 1–11	30	7	37
Leicester Number Tests	3	–	3
Manchester Reading Comprehension Test (Senior)	1	–	1

Name of Test	Secondary	Middle	Total
Mill Hill Vocabulary Scale	3	–	3
Nicholls Framework for Reading	2	–	2
The Neale Analysis of Reading Ability	69	7	76
NFER			
Verbal Test EF	2	–	2
Non-Verbal BD	–	1	1
Non-Verbal DH	32	–	32
English Progress Test D2	1	–	1
Reading Test AD	2	–	2
Reading Comprehension Test DE	3	–	3
Reading Test EH 1-2	3	–	3
Welsh Sentence Reading	1	–	1
Mathematics Attainment Test C1	1	–	1
Basic Mathematics Test DE	5	–	5
AH2 Group Test of General Ability	3	–	3
AH3 Group Test of General Ability	2	–	2
Profile of Mathematical Skills (France)	6	–	6
Oliver and Boyd Maths Tests 1–20	1	–	1
Raven's Standard Progressive Matrices	27	3	30
Richmond Tests of Basic Skills Levels 1–6	15	5	20
Rutter's Children's Behaviour Rating Scale	1	–	1
Salford Sentence Reading Test	4	–	4
Schonell Tests			
R1 Graded Word Reading Test	26	3	29
R2 Simple Prose Reading Test	1	–	1
R3 Silent Reading Test A }	16	–	16
R4 Silent Reading Test B }			
R5 Test of Analysis and Synthesis of			
Words Containing Common Phonic Units	1	–	1
Essential Intelligence Test	2	–	2
Essential Mechanical Arithmetic Test	2	–	2
Simplex Junior Intelligence Scale	1	–	1
Southgate Group Reading Tests			
Test 1 Word Selection Test }	2	–	2
Test 2 Sentence Completion Test }			
Spar Reading Test (Young)	4	–	4
Spar Spelling Test (Young)	7	–	7

Name of Test	Secondary	Middle	Total
Spooncer Group Reading Assessment	1	–	1
Swansea Test of Phonic Skills	5	–	5
Tansley Spelling Cards	2	–	2
Vernon Arithmetic Test	7	–	7
Wechsler Intelligence Scale for Children (WISC) – Revised	1	–	1
Wepman Auditory Discrimination Test	5	–	5
Widespan Reading Test	6	–	6
Yardsticks . . . Criterion-Referenced Tests in Mathematics	2	–	2
Young Non-Readers Intelligence Test	8	–	8
Young Group Mathematics Test	2	–	2
Young Reading Test	7	–	7

Note
Other tests for which insufficient details
were recorded for references to be given.

	Secondary	Middle	Total
Tests of language skills	9	–	9
Tests of dyslexia	5	1	6
Tests of number skills	11	–	11
Other unspecified tests	24	2	26
	49	3	52

Appendix 3A.3: *Tests used to investigate slow learners with behavioural/emotional problems*

Name of Test	Schools Using Test		
	Secondary	Middle	Total
Aston Index	6	–	6
Bristol Achievement Tests: English Language	1	1	2
Bristol Social Adjustment Guide	48	5	53
Cotswold Personality Assessment	1	–	1
Eysenck Personality Inventory	5	–	5
Draw-A-Man Test (Goodenough–Harris Drawing Test)	1	–	1
Jesness Inventory	1	–	1
Manchester Scales of Social Adaptation	1	–	1
Neale Analysis of Reading Ability	1	1	2
New Junior Maudsley Inventory	1	–	1
Rothwell–Miller Interest Blank	1	–	1
Rutter Children's Behaviour Rating Scale	6	–	6
Schonell Essential Intelligence Test	1	–	1
Webster Diagnostic Test for Dyslexia	1	–	1
Wechsler Intelligence Scale for Children (WISC) – Revised	1	–	1

Note

Other tests in Appendix 3 for which insufficient detail was recorded for a reference to be given.

	6	–	6

Appendix 5A.1: *Teaching experience of those who taught slow learners (N=1449)*

Type of Teaching Experience	No. of Teachers	
	N	%
Infant, Junior and Middle (JMI)	40	(3)
Middle, Infant and Special	3	(neg.)
Middle	31	(2)
Junior, Middle, Infant and Secondary	419	(29)
Secondary	696	(48)
Special	3	(neg.)
Secondary and Special	51	(4)
Junior, Middle, Infant, Secondary and Special	98	(7)
Other teaching experience, e.g. Forces, Other Combinations	108	(7)
	1449	(100)

No response – 18

Appendix 5A.2: *Training of those who taught slow learners.*[1] *(N=1420)*

Type of Training Course	Course Unit on Slow Learners Number of Teachers					
	Yes	%	No.	%	Total	%
Infant	11	(24)	34	(76)	45	(3)
Junior	90	(33)	187	(67)	277	(20)
Middle	66	(46)	77	(56)	143	(10)
Infant, Junior and Middle	20	(50)	20	(50)	40	(3)
Infant, Junior and Secondary	43	(26)	121	(74)	164	(11)
Secondary	158	(25)	470	(75)	628	(44)
Secondary and Middle	11	(28)	28	(72)	39	(3)
Other kinds of training, e.g. special, other combinations	30	(36)	54	(64)	84	(6)
	429		991		1420	(100)

[1] 32 teachers had received no training.
No response – 15

Appendix 5A.3: *Perceived importance of special training for teaching slow learners*

	Importance of Specialist Training				
	Essential	Very Important	Not Very Important	Not Necessary At All	Total
Teachers with					
special training	116	245	55	4	420
no special training	276	516	152	12	956
no teacher training	11	22	7	2	42
	403	783	214	18	1418
	(29%)	(55%)	(15%)	(1%)	(100%)

No response – 49

Appendix 5A.4: *Main subjects studied by staff with degrees*

Main Subjects	No. of Staff				Totals
	B.Ed.	B.A./B.Sc.	Masters[1]	N	N=298
English	14	19	5	38	58 (20)
English + one other subject	12	7	1	20	
Maths	2	8	1	11	17 (6)
Maths + one other subject	3	3	–	6	
Science	5	15	–	20	23 (8)
Science + one other subject	2	1	–	3	
Geography	5	12	1	18	25 (8)
Geography + one other subject	5	2	–	7	
History	8	17	–	25	33 (11)
History + one other subject	7	1	–	8	
RE	3	2	–	5	7 (2)
RE + one other subject	–	2	–	2	
Art, Craft, Design	3	–	–	3	4 (1)
Art, Craft, Design + one other subject	1	–	–	1	
PE	5	–	–	5	6 (2)
PE + one other subject	1	–	–	1	
Psychology	2	10	–	12	18 (6)
Psychology + one other subject	3	3	–	6	
Sociology	1	5	–	6	10 (3)
Sociology + one other subject	3	1	–	4	
Economics	–	5	–	5	6 (2)
Economics + one other subject	–	1	–	1	
Humanities/Social Science	2	7	–	9	13 (4)
Humanities/Social Science + one other subject	1	3	–	4	
Modern Languages	1	10	–	11	14 (5)
Modern Languages + one other subject	1	2	–	3	
Education	3	12	2	17	17 (6)
Special Education	6	2	–	8	8 (3)
General Subjects	2	7	–	9	9 (3)
Other subjects, e.g. Geology, Drama, Classics, Politics, Technology, Music	9	19	2	30	30 (10)
	110	176	12		298 (100)

[1] One Ph.D. is included in this column.

Appendix 5A.5: *Main subjects studied by staff with teachers' certificates (Cert.Ed.)*

Main Subjects	Number of Staff	Totals N	%
English	88 ⎞	120	(23)
English + one other subject	32 ⎠		
Maths	33 ⎞	46	(9)
Maths + one other subject	13 ⎠		
Science	31 ⎞	43	(9)
Science + one other subject	12 ⎠		
Geography	49 ⎞	57	(11)
Geography + one other subject	8 ⎠		
History	41 ⎞	49	(9)
History + one other subject	8 ⎠		
RE	24 ⎞	28	(5)
RE + one other subject	4 ⎠		
Art, Craft and Design	42 ⎞	48	(9)
Art, Craft and Design + one other subject	6 ⎠		
PE	34 ⎞	56	(11)
PE + one other subject	22 ⎠		
Music		14	(3)
Home Economics		12	(3)
General Subjects		22	(4)
Other subjects, e.g. Sociology, Economics, Drama		21	(4)
		516	(100)

Pupil	Number in Group	Age	Type of Provision for Slow Learners	Length of Lesson Observed	Individual Working with Teacher		Group Working with Teacher		Class Activities with Teacher		Pupil Working alone on Individual Activities		Pupil Working alone on Class Activities		Pupil "off task" during lesson	
				min.	min.	%	min.	%	min.	%	min.	%	min.	%	min.	%
Carol	1	11+	Withdrawal	35	35	(100)	–		–		–		–		–	
Vincent	1	13+	Withdrawal	50	50	(100)	–		–		–		–		–	
Paul	3	11+	Withdrawal	50	30	(60)	–		–		20	(40)	–		–	
Mary	4	11+	Withdrawal	70	20	(28)	25	(36)	–		25	(36)	–		–	
Malcolm	4	12+	Withdrawal	60	22	(37)	–		–		38	(63)	–		–	
Peter	7	11+	Withdrawal	65	13	(20)	9	(14)	–		43	(66)	–		–	
Mark	8	11+	Withdrawal	52	13	(25)	–		–		39	(75)	–		–	
Paul	9	11+	Special Class	35	–		–		–		–		35	(100)	–	
Malcolm	10	12+	Special Class	65	8	(12)	–		15	(23)	–		42	(65)	–	
Harry	13	11+	Special Class	100	–		–		65	(65)	–		35	(35)	–	
Penny	14	11+	Special Class	35	–		–		5	(14)	20	(57)	10	(29)	–	
Philip	14	11+	Special Class	115	2	(2)	–		9	(8)	–		104	(90)	–	
Helen	15	11+	Set	65	5	(8)	–		30	(46)	30	(46)	–		–	
Alan	16	11+	Set	60	–		–		35	(58)	20	(33)	–		5	(8)
Steven	16	11+	Special Class	70	5	(7)	–		3	(4)	62	(89)	–		–	
Steven	16	11+	Special Class	60	2	(3)	–		14	(23)	–		44	(73)	–	
Michael	17	11+	Special Class	70	–		–		35	(50)	–		35	(50)	–	
Karen	18	11+	Special Class	75	3	(4)	–		40	(53)	–		32	(43)	–	
Alan	18	11+	Set	60	–		–		25	(42)	–		35	(58)	–	

Appendix 6A.2: *Patterns of classroom organization observed during maths/numeracy lessons*

Pupil	Number in Group	Age	Type of Provision	Length of Lesson Observed	Time (in minutes) and percentage of lesson									
					Individual Working with Teacher		Class Activities with Teacher		Pupil Working alone on Individual Activities		Pupil Working alone on Class Activities		Pupil "Off task" during lesson	
				min.	min.	%	min.	%	min.	%	min.	%	min.	%
Malcolm	10	12+	Set	65	3	(5)	–	–	62	(95)	–		60	(92)
Heather	13	11+	Special Class	65	2	(3)	–	–	63	(97)	–		40	(61)
Helen	13	11+	Set	42	6	(14)	–	–	36	(86)	–		27	(64)
Fred	16	12+	Set	50	3	(6)	–	–	47	(94)	–		4	(8)
Michael	17	11+	Special Class	55	4	(7)	–	–	51	(93)	–		39	(71)
Peter	27	11+	Mixed Ability	65	–		5	(8)	60	(92)	–		42	(65)
William	12	13+	Special Class	60	–		7	(12)	53	(88)	–		8	(13)
Carol	27	11+	Mixed Ability	30	4	(13)	–		–		26	(87)	7	(23)
Penny	14	11+	Special Class	65	2	(3)	25	(38)	–		38	(59)	–	
Stella	19	11+	Set	65	5	(8)	40	(62)	–		20	(30)	12	(18)
Mark	20	11+	Set	50	1	(2)	27	(54)	–		22	(44)	–	
Henry	21	12+	Slow Learner Set	65	–		32	(49)	–		33	(51)	5	(8)
Karen	18	11+	Special	85	–		63	(74)	–		22	(26)	–	

Bibliography

ATHEY, L. (1978). 'Current provision for remedial education in Welsh secondary schools', *Remedial Education*, 13, 3.

BAILEY, T.J. (1981). 'The secondary remedial teacher's role redefined', *Remedial Education*, 16, 3.

BENNETT, N. (1976). *Teaching Styles and Pupil Progress*. London: Open Books.

BULLOCK REPORT. GREAT BRITAIN. DEPARTMENT OF EDUCATION AND SCIENCE (1975). *A Language for Life*. London: HMSO.

BRENNAN, W.K. (1974). *Shaping the education of slow learners*. London: Routledge & Kegan Paul.

BRENNAN, W.K. (1979). *Curricular needs of slow learners*. (Schools Council Working Paper 63.) London: Evans/Methuen.

COOPER REPORT. GREAT BRITAIN. DEPARTMENT OF EDUCATION AND SCIENCE (1981). *'School-Industry Link Schemes: a study and recommendations'*. London: HMSO.

COX, C.B. and BOYSON, R. (1977). *Black Paper*. London: Maurice Temple Smith.

EVANS, T. (1976). 'Teaching Children of Mixed Ability', *Special Education*, 3,3.

GAINS, C. (1978). *'Questions of Definition'*, *Times Educational Supplement*, 22nd September.

GAINS, C. and McNICHOLAS, M. (1981). *'Broader remedies'*, *Times Educational Supplement*, 11th September.

GREAT BRITAIN. DEPARTMENT OF EDUCATION AND SCIENCE (1971). *Slow Learners in Secondary Schools*. Education Survey 15. London: HMSO.

GREAT BRITAIN. DEPARTMENT OF EDUCATION AND SCIENCE (1977). *Curriculum 11–16*. London: HMSO.

GREAT BRITAIN. DEPARTMENT OF EDUCATION AND SCIENCE (1977). *Ten Good Schools: A Secondary School Enquiry*. London: HMSO.

GREAT BRITAIN. DEPARTMENT OF EDUCATION AND SCIENCE (1979). *Aspects of Secondary Education in England*. London: HMSO.

GREAT BRITAIN. DEPARTMENT OF EDUCATION AND SCIENCE (1979). *Statistics of Education*, no. 4, 'Teachers' (England and Wales). London: HMSO.

GREAT BRITAIN. DEPARTMENT OF EDUCATION AND SCIENCE (1981). *'School–Industry Link Schemes: a study and recommendations'*. London: HMSO.

GULLIFORD, R. (1971). *Special Educational Needs*. London: Routledge and Kegan Paul.

LAWRENCE, D. (1976). 'Same, but different?', *Times Educational Supplement*, 2nd July.

McCALL, C. (1977). 'Remedial strategies in secondary schools', *Forum*, 19, 2.

NATIONAL ASSOCIATION FOR REMEDIAL EDUCATION (NARE) (1979). *Guidelines 2*. Stafford: NARE.

NATFHE (1978). (BULLOCK, J.F. (Ed)) *Handbook of Institutions providing both Teacher Training and other full-time Advanced Courses England and Wales.*

O'HAGAN, F.J. (1977). 'The role of the remedial teacher: problems and perspectives', *Remedial Education*, 12, 2.

PUMFREY, P.D. (1976). *Reading Tests and Assessment Techniques.* London: Hodder & Stoughton.

REID, M., CLUNIES-ROSS, L., GOACHER, B. and VILE, C. (1981). *Mixed Ability Teaching: Problems and Possibilities.* Windsor: NFER-Nelson.

RUTTER, M., MAUGHAN, B., MORTIMORE, P. and OUSTON, J. (1979). *Fifteen Thousand Hours.* London: Open Books.

SAMPSON, O.C. (1975). *Remedial Education.* London: Routledge & Kegan Paul.

SAMPSON, O.C. and PUMFREY P.D. (1970). 'A Study of Remedial Education in the Secondary stage of Schooling', *Remedial Education*, 5, 3.

SCHOOLS COUNCIL (1981). Working Paper 70: *The Practical Curriculum.* London: Methuen Educational.

STEWART, N. (1977). 'WSSA Enquiry on Remedial Education in Welsh Secondary Schools', *Welsh Secondary Schools Review*, 64, 2.

WARNOCK REPORT. GREAT BRITAIN. DEPARTMENT OF EDUCATION AND SCIENCE (1978). *Special Educational Needs.* London: HMSO.

WILLIAMS, A.A. (1970). *'Basic Subjects for Slow Learners'.* London: Methuen.

YOUNG, D. (1976). *Spar Reading Test.* London: Hodder & Stoughton Educational.

List of tests used by schools in the survey

(Authors' names are given in parentheses)

APU ARITHMETIC TEST (Closs, S.J. and Hutchings, M.) (1979–80). London: Hodder & Stoughton.

ASTON INDEX (Newton, M. and Thomson, M.) (1975). Wisbech: Learning Development Aids.

BASIC NUMBER SCREENING TEST (Gillham, W.E.C. and Hesse, K.A.) (1976). London: Hodder & Stoughton.

BLACKWELL'S SPELLING TEST (Sadler, B.R. and Page, E.G.) (1980). Oxford: Blackwell.

BRISTOL ACHIEVEMENT TESTS: ENGLISH LANGUAGE (Brimer A. and Gross, H.) (1969). Windsor: NFER:Nelson.

BRISTOL ACHIEVEMENT TESTS: MATHEMATICS (Brimer, A.) (1969). Windsor: NFER-Nelson.

BRISTOL SOCIAL ADJUSTMENT GUIDES (Scott, D.H., Maston, N.C. and Sykes, E.G.) (1956–1966). London: University of London Press.

BURT RE-ARRANGED WORD READING TEST (Burt, C.) (1938). London: University of London Press.

BURT WORD READING TEST (Burt, C.) (1974, revised 1976). London:

Hodder & Stoughton, for Scottish Council for Research in Education.

CARVER'S WORD RECOGNITION TEST (Carver, C.) (1970). London: University of London Press.

CASSELL LINKED ENGLISH TESTS: ATTAINMENT TEST (Higgins, D.S.) (1977). London: Cassell.

CHILDREN'S BEHAVIOUR RATING SCALE (Rutter, M.) (1964–65). London: Institute of Psychiatry.

COGNITIVE ABILITIES TEST (Thorndike, R.L. and Hagen, E.) (1973). Windsor: NFER-Nelson.

CORNWELL ORALLY PRESENTED GROUP TEST OF INTELLIGENCE FOR JUNIORS (Cornwell, J.) (1952). London: Methuen.

COTTERELL CHECK LIST OF BASIC SOUNDS (Cotterell, G.) (1974). Wisbech: Learning Development Aids.

COTSWOLD PERSONALITY ASSESSMENT (Fleming, C.M.) (1960). Glasgow: Gibson.

CRICHTON VOCABULARY SCALE (Raven, J.C.) (1950). London: Lewis.

CULTURE FAIR INTELLIGENCE TESTS (Cattell, R.B. and Cattell, A.K.S.) (1960–61). Indianapolis: Bobbs–Merrill.

DANIELS AND DIACK STANDARD READING TESTS: TEST 1, THE STANDARD TEST OF READING SKILL (Daniels, J.C. and Diack, H.) (1958). St Albans: Hart–Davis Educational.

DANIELS AND DIACK STANDARD READING TESTS: TEST 11, GRADED SPELLING TEST (Daniels, J.C. and Diack, H.) (1958). St. Albans: Hart–Davis Educational.

DANIELS AND DIACK STANDARD READING TESTS: TEST 12, GRADED TEST OF READING EXPERIENCE (Daniels, J.C. and Diack, H.) (1958). St. Albans: Hart–Davis Educational.

DIAGNOSTIC AND REMEDIAL SPELLING MANUAL (Peters, M.R.) (1975). Basingstoke: Macmillan.

DIAGNOSTIC TEST FOR DYSLEXIA (Webster, J.) (1972). Aylesbury: Ginn.

DOMAIN PHONIC TESTS (McLeod, J. and Atkinson, J.) (1972). Edinburgh: Oliver & Boyd.

DORCAN SPELLING ANALYSIS (Dobinson, H.H.) (1979). Walton-on-Thames: Nelson.

DRAW-A-MAN TEST (*See* Goodenough–Harris Drawing Test).

EDINBURGH READING TESTS (The Godfrey Thomson Unit, University of Edinburgh) (1972–73). London: Hodder & Stoughton.

ENGLISH PICTURE VOCABULARY TEST (Brimer, M.A. and Dunn, L.M.) (1962–68). England: Educational Evaluation Enterprises.

EYSENCK PERSONALITY INVENTORY (Eysenck, H.J. and Eysenck, S.B.G.) (1963–69). London: University of London Press.

FRAMEWORK FOR READING (Dean, J. and Nicols, R.) (1974). London: Evans.

FROSTIG DEVELOPMENTAL TEST OF VISUAL PERCEPTION (Frostig, M. *et al.*) (1961–66). Palo Alto, California: Consulting Psychologists Press.

GAP READING COMPREHENSION TEST (McLeod, J.) (1965–70). London: Heinemann.

GAPADOL (McLeod, J. and Anderson, J.) (1972). London: Heinemann.

GATES–MACGINITIE READING TESTS (Gates, A.I. and MacGinitie, W.H.) (1926–72). New York: Teachers College Press.

GATES–McKILLOP READING DIAGNOSTIC TESTS (Gates, A.I. and McKillop, A.S.) (1926–62). New York: Teachers College Press.

GOODENOUGH–HARRIS DRAWING TEST (Goodenough, F.L. and Harris, D.B.) (1926–63). London: Harcourt Brace Jovanovich.

HARRIS TESTS OF LATERAL DOMINANCE (Harris, A.J.) (1947–58). New York: Psychological Corporation.

HILLINGDON MODULES (*See* Transitional Assessment Modules)

HOLBORN READING SCALE (Watts, A.F.) (Revision of 1948 edition) (1980). London: Harrap.

JESNESS INVENTORY (Jesness, C.F.) (1966–72). Palo Alto, California: Consulting Psychologists Press.

KINGSTON TEST OF SILENT READING (Hebron, M.E.) (1953–54), London: Harrap.

LEICESTER NUMBER TEST (Gillam, G. and Hesse, K.A.) (1968). London: University of London Press.

LONDON READING TEST (Biscoe, M. and others in collaboration with ILEA Research and Statistics Group) (1978). Windsor: NFER-Nelson.

MANCHESTER READING COMPREHENSION TEST (SENIOR) (Wiseman, S. and Wrigley, J.) (1959). London: University of London Press.

MANCHESTER SCALES OF SOCIAL ADAPTATION (Lunger, E.A.) (1966). Windsor: NFER-Nelson.

MILL HILL VOCABULARY SCALE (Raven, J.C.) (1943). London: H.K. Lewis.

MORAY HOUSE TESTS (*See* Edinburgh Reading Tests)

NEALE ANALYSIS OF READING ABILITY (Neale, M.O.) (1970). (2nd edition) London: Macmillan.

NEW JUNIOR MAUDSLEY INVENTORY (Furneaux, W.D. and Gibson, H.B.) (1961–67). London: University of London Press.

NFER VERBAL TEST CD (Land, C.) (1977). Windsor: NFER-Nelson.

NFER VERBAL TEST D (Postlethwaite, T.N.) (1970). Windsor: NFER-Nelson.

NFER VERBAL TEST EF (Wood, O. and Land, V.) (1970). Windsor: NFER-Nelson.

NFER VERBAL TEST GH (Land, V.) (1966). (Test restandardised in 1978). Windsor: NFER-Nelson.

NFER NON-VERBAL BD (Pidgeon, D.A.) (1964). Windsor: NFER-Nelson.

NFER NON-VERBAL DH (Calvert, B.) (1978). Windsor: NFER-Nelson.

NFER AH2 GROUP TEST OF GENERAL ABILITY (Heim, A.W., Watts, K.P. and Simmonds, V.) (1975). Windsor: NFER-Nelson.

NFER AH3 GROUP TEST OF GENERAL ABILITY (Heim, A.W., Watts, K.P. and Simmonds, V.) (1975). Windsor: NFER-Nelson.

NFER AH4 GROUP TEST OF GENERAL INTELLIGENCE (Heim, A.W.) (1968). (Regular edition). Windsor: NFER-Nelson.

NFER READING TESTS SR–A AND SR–B (Pre-1958). (Restricted tests). Windsor: NFER-Nelson.

NFER READING TEST AD (Watts, A.F.) (1970). Windsor: NFER-Nelson.

NFER WELSH SENTENCE READING TEST (Evans, G.J.) (1959). Prawf Darlien Branddegau 1. Windsor: NFER-Nelson.

NFER READING TEST BD (1971). Windsor: NFER-Nelson.

NFER READING COMPREHENSION TEST DE (Barnard, B.) (1974). Windsor: NFER-Nelson.

NFER READING TEST EH 1–2 (Bate, S.M.) (1975). (New standardization 1979). Windsor: NFER-Nelson.

NFER ENGLISH PROGRESS TEST C2 (Land, V.) (1960). Windsor: NFER-Nelson.

NFER ENGLISH PROGRESS TEST D2 (Henchman, J.) (1962–64). Winsor: NFER-Nelson.

NFER MATHEMATICS ATTAINMENT TEST B (1977). Windsor: NFER-Nelson.

NFER MATHEMATICS ATTAINMENT TEST C1 (1977). Windsor: NFER-Nelson.

NFER MATHEMATICS ATTAINMENT TEST DE1 (1967). Windsor: NFER-Nelson.

NFER BASIC MATHEMATICS TEST A (1975). Windsor: NFER-Nelson.

NFER BASIC MATHEMATICS TEST B (1971). Windsor: NFER-Nelson.

NFER BASIC MATHEMATICS TEST DE (1974). Windsor: NFER-Nelson.

OLIVER AND BOYD MATHS TEST 1–20 (1977). Edinburgh: Oliver & Boyd.

OTIS–LENNON MENTAL ABILITY TESTS (Otis, A.S. and Lennon, R.T.) (1937–54). London: Harcourt Brace Jovanovich.

PHONIC SKILLS TESTS 1–11 (Jackson, S.) (1971). Glasgow: Gibson.

PROFILE OF MATHEMATICAL SKILLS (France, N.) (1979). London: Nelson, Department of Measurement and Guidance.

RAVEN'S STANDARD PROGRESSIVE MATRICES (Raven, J.C.) (1938–56). Windsor: NFER-Nelson.

RICHMOND TESTS OF BASIC SKILLS (LEVELS 1–6) (1974). Windsor: NFER-Nelson.

ROTHWELL–MILLER INTEREST BLANK (Miller, K.M. and Rothwell, J.W.) (1968–68). Hawthorn, Victoria: ACER.

SALFORD SENTENCE READING TEST (1976). London: Hodder & Stoughton.

SCHONELL READING TESTS, R1 GRADED WORD READING TEST (Schonell, F.J.) (1942–55). Edinburgh: Oliver & Boyd.

SCHONELL READING TESTS, R2 SIMPLE PROSE READING TEST (Schonell, F.J.) (1942–55). Edinburgh: Oliver & Boyd.

SCHONELL READING TESTS, R3 SILENT READING TEST A AND R4 SILENT READING TEST B (Schonell, R.J.) (1942–55). Edinburgh: Oliver & Boyd.

SCHONELL READING TESTS, R5 TEST OF ANALYSIS AND SYNTHESIS OF WORDS CONTAINING COMMON PHONIC UNITS (1942–55). Edinburgh: Oliver & Boyd.

SCHONELL GRADED WORD SPELLING TEST S1 OR S2 (Schonell, F.J.) (1942–56). Edinburgh: Oliver & Boyd.

SCHONELL DIAGNOSTIC ENGLISH TEST 5, COMPOSITION (Schonell, F.J.) (Pre-1950). Edinburgh: Oliver & Boyd.

SCHONELL ESSENTIAL INTELLIGENCE TEST (Schonell, F.J. and Adams, R.H.) (1940). Edinburgh: Oliver & Boyd.

SCHONELL ESSENTIAL MECHANICAL ARITHMETIC TEST (Schonell, F.J.) (Pre-1950). Edinburgh: Oliver & Boyd.

SIMPLEX JUNIOR INTELLIGENCE SCALE (Richardson, C.A.) (1932–51). London: Harrap.

SOUTHGATE GROUP READING TESTS, TEST 1 WORD SELECTION TEST, TEST 2 SENTENCE COMPLETION TEST (Southgate, V.) Test 1 (1960–61). Test 2 (1962). London: University of London Press.

SPAR READING TEST (Young, D.) (1976). London: Hodder & Stoughton.

SPAR SPELLING TEST (Young, D.) (1976). London: Hodder & Stoughton.

SPELLING CARDS (Tansley, A.E.) (1978). London: E.J. Arnold.

SPOONCER GROUP READING ASSESSMENT (Spooncer, F.A.) (1964). London: University of London Press.

SWANSEA TEST OF PHONIC SKILLS (Williams, P., *et al.* (1970–71). Oxford: Basil Blackwell for Schools Council Research and Development Project in Compensatory Education.

TRANSITIONAL ASSESSMENT MODULES (1978). Windsor: NFER-Nelson. (NFER and London Borough of Hillingdon).

VERNON GRADED ARITHMETIC TEST (Vernon, P.E.) (1970). London: Hodder & Stoughton.

VERNON GRADED WORD READING TEST (Vernon, P.E.) (1938). London: Hodder & Stoughton.

WEPMAN AUDITORY DISCRIMINATION TEST (Wepman, J.M.) (Revised 1973). Chicago, Illinois: Language Research Associates.

WECHSLER INTELLIGENCE SCALE FOR CHILDREN (WISC) – REVISED (Wechsler, D.) (1974). Windsor: NFER-Nelson.

WIDESPAN READING TEST (Brimer, A.) (1972). Windsor: NFER-Nelson.

YARDSTICKS (CRITERION-REFERENCED TESTS IN MATHEMATICS) (1975). Windsor: NFER-Nelson.

YOUNG GROUP MATHEMATICS TEST (Young, D.) (1970). London: University of London Press.

YOUNG GROUP READING TEST (Young, D.) (1969). London: Hodder & Stoughton.

YOUNG NON-READERS INTELLIGENCE TEST (Young, D.) (1964). London: University of London Press.

Index